The Fox & Hubbard
Families of Indiana, Arkansas
England & Gernany

Gary Fox

Tennessee Research Company 2018
306 West Rockwood St
Rockwood TN 37854

Dedication

Dear Family,
Over the past three years of working independently, and then hiring help from a professional Genealogist, I have completed our family history to the best of my ability.
The research in this book was done by using public documents, such as census, marriage, birth and death records with various Ancestry Databases. I made many research contacts at Texas Archives in which I received historic information and documented papers that I scanned into various records.
I am thankful to all my past and present family members who were so kind to me whenever I asked for help confirming my questions.
I hope you find this book interesting.
Yours Truly
May 2017

Abbreviations

ABBREVIATIONS

DAR Daughters of the American Revolution

SAR Sons of the American Revolution

FFA First Families of America

SCV Sons of Confederate Veterans

UDC United Daughters of the Confederacy

SDT Sons and Daughters of Texas

NOTE: The older family members are direct lines back brother and sisters are omitted for space reasons only.

Table of Contents

Table of Contents

Family Tree Chart for Gary Fox

Chart no. 1

8 Charles Wesley Fox   cont. 2
b. 9 Sep 1857
p. Cincinatti, Hamilton County Ohio
m. 8 Sep 1881
p. Crittenden County, Kentucky
d. 27 Aug 1927
p. Livingston, Crittenden County, Kentucky

9 Juliet Hodge   cont. 3
b. 18 Apr 1860
p. Crittenden County, Kentucky
d. 20 Apr 1925
p. Crittenden County, Kentucky

4 Vernon Richard Fox
b. 2 May 1884
p. Lebanon, Marion County, Kentucky
m. 1909
p. Crittenden County Kentucky
d. May 1968
p. Manila, Mississippi County Arkansas

10 Marion Forrest Pogue   cont. 4
b. 18 Oct 1867
p. Crittenden County Kentucky
m. 18 Apr 1887
p. Crittenden County Kentucky
d. 26 Sep 1952
p. Caldwell County Kentucky

11 Bettie Florence Matthews   cont. 5
b. 10 Nov 1868
p. Crittenden County Kentucky
d. 29 Feb 1952
p. Caldwell County Kentucky

5 Clara Augusta Pogue
b. 12 May 1888
p. Crittenden County Kentucky
d. Aug 1936
p. Manila, Mississippi County Arkansas

2 William Garrad Fox
b. 21 Aug 1918
p. Manila, Mississippi County, Arkansas
m. 20 Feb 1943
p. Detroit, Wayne, Michigan
d. 14 Nov 2007
p. Lenoir City, Loudon County, Tennessee

1 Gary Fox
b.
p.
m.
p.
d.
p.
sp. Barbara Jean Sinclair

12 Thomas Hubbard   cont. 6
b. 4 Dec 1874
p. Pigeon, Vanderburgh County, Indiana
m.
p.
d. 30 Jul 1939
p. Evansville, Vanderburgh, Indiana

13 Lena Laubner   cont. 7
b. 8 Jul 1876
p. Indiana
d. 28 Sep 1938
p. Evansville, Vanderburgh County, Indiana

6 Marvin Dean Hubbard
b. 11 Mar 1903
p. Evansville, Vanderburgh County, Indiana
m.
p.
d. 16 Dec 1963
p. Evansville, Vanderburgh County, Indiana

3 Marion Francis Hubbard
b. 17 Dec 1923
p. Evansville, Vanderburgh County, Indiana
d. 3 Mar 2012
p. Lenoir City Loudon County Tennessee

14 Jacob Wagner   cont. 8
b. Mar 1863
p. Elberfeld, Warrick County, Indiana
m.
p.
d. 11 Mar 1931
p. Elberfeld, Warrick County, Indiana

15 Julia M. Pfingston   cont. 9
b. 5 Feb 1870
p. Germany
d. 18 Mar 1958
p. Evansville, Vanderburgh County, Indiana

7 Lydia Wagner
b. 1900
p. Campbell, Warrick County, Indiana
d. 1957
p. Manila, Mississippi County, Arkansas

No. 1 on this chart is the same as no. 8 on chart no. 1

8 Thomas Fox　　　　cont. 10
b. Abt 1739
p. Doncaster, Yorkshire, England
m. 14 Jun 1767
p. Yorkshire, England
d. 19 Sep 1801
p. Finningley, Yorkshire, England

9 Sarah Walker　　　　cont. 11
b. 1742
p. Fishlake, Yorkshire, England
d. 19 Jun 1827
p. Finningley, Yorkshire, England

4 George Fox
b. 3 Sep 1775
p. Finningly, Yorkshire, , England
m. 14 Nov 1799
p. Barnsley, Yorkshire, England
d. 16 Apr 1845
p. Hamilton County Ohio

2 John Wesley Fox
b. Abt 1815-1820
p. Hamilton County Ohio
m. Abt 1842
p. Hamilton County Ohio
d. Aft 1880
p. Crittenden County Kentucky

10
b.
p.
m.
p.
d.
p.

11
b.
p.
d.
p.

5 Addy Jackson
b. 1775
p.
d. 4 Mar 1819
p. Hamilton County Ohio

1 Charles Wesley Fox
b. 9 Sep 1857
p. Cincinatti, Hamilton County Ohio
m. 8 Sep 1881
p. Crittenden County, Kentucky
d. 27 Aug 1927
p. Livingston, Crittenden County, Kentucky
sp. Juliet Hodge

12
b.
p.
m.
p.
d.
p.

13
b.
p.
d.
p.

6
b.
p.
m.
p.
d.
p.

3 Elizabeth King
b. Abt 1825
p. Hamilton County Ohio
d. Bef 1869
p. Cincinnati, Hamilton County Ohio

14
b.
p.
m.
p.
d.
p.

7
b.
p.
d.
p.

15
b.
p.
d.
p.

Family Tree Chart for Juliet Hodge

No. 1 on this chart is the same as no. 9 on chart no. 1

8 Henry Harry Hodge   cont. 12
b. Abt 1745
p. North Carolina
m. Bef 1777
p.
d. 10 Feb 1824
p. Livingston County Kentucky

9 Catherine Bryant
b. 1752
p. North Carolina
d. Abt 1794
p. Livingston County Kentucky

4 William Fidella Hodge
b. 1777
p. Edgecombe County North Carolina
m.
p.
d. 1826
p. Livingston County Kentucky

2 Asel Branson Hodge
b. 18 Jan 1825
p. Livingston County Kentucky
m.
p.
d. 4 Jan 1889
p. Crittenden County Kentucky

5 Nancy Josiphine Dancy
b.
p.
d.
p.

10
b.
p.
m.
p.
d.
p.

11
b.
p.
d.
p.

1 Juliet Hodge
b. 18 Apr 1860
p. Crittenden County, Kentucky
m. 8 Sep 1881
p. Crittenden County, Kentucky
d. 20 Apr 1925
p. Crittenden County, Kentucky
sp. Charles Wesley Fox

12
b.
p.
m.
p.
d.
p.

6 Solomon Millikan
b. 28 Feb 1784
p. Grainger County Tennessee
m. 1 Aug 1804
p. Grainger County Tennessee
d. 26 Oct 1860
p. Crittenden County Kentucky

13
b.
p.
d.
p.

3 Catharine Elizabeth Millikan
b. 16 Oct 1829
p. Grainger County Tennessee
d. 18 Dec 1889
p. Crittenden County Kentucky

14
b.
p.
m.
p.
d.
p.

7 Nancy Morgan
b. 1783
p. Grainger County Tennessee
d. 1865
p. Crittenden County Kentucky

15
b.
p.
d.
p.

No. 1 on this chart is the same as no. 10 on chart no. 1

Chart no. 4

8 William Thomas Pogue   cont. 13
b. 8 Feb 1783
p. Pocahontas County Virginia now West Vir~
m.
p.
d. 27 May 1827
p. Tazwell County Virginia

4 Thomas Franklin Pogue
b. 21 Jan 1802
p. Tazwell County Virginia
m. 26 Dec 1844
p. Graves County Kentucky
d. 20 Jun 1857
p. Calloway County, Kentucky

9 Mary
b. 1784
p. Virginia
d.
p.

2 William Washington Pogue
b. 11 Dec 1845
p. Murray, Calloway County, Kentucky
m. 19 Dec 1866
p. Crittenden County Kentucky
d. 5 Mar 1926
p. Crittenden County Kentucky

10 Jonathan Cruise
b. Abt 1790
p. Greenville County South Carolina
m.
p.
d. Oct 1864
p. Crittenden County Kentucky

5 Harriet Cruise
b. 11 May 1823
p. North Carolina
d. 1 Dec 1892
p. Calloway County, Kentucky

11 Holly Bennett
b. Abt 1794
p. Madison County Kentucky
d. Bef 1850
p. Calloway County Kentucky

1 Marion Forrest Pogue
b. 18 Oct 1867
p. Crittenden County Kentucky
m. 18 Apr 1887
p. Crittenden County Kentucky
d. 26 Sep 1952
p. Caldwell County Kentucky
sp. Bettie Florence Matthews

12 Walter Oliver
b.
p.
m.
p.
d.
p.

6 Henry W. Oliver
b. 7 Oct 1816
p. Virginia
m. 2 Sep 1847
p. Trigg County Kentucky
d. 11 May 1873
p. Crittenden County Kentucky

13 Mary Cox Winn
b.
p.
d.
p.

3 Mary Catherine Oliver
b. 22 Jul 1849
p. Crittenden County Kentucky
d. 14 Apr 1939
p. Crittenden County Kentucky

14 William Rolston
b.
p.
m.
p.
d.
p.

7 Margaret C. Rolston
b. 6 Jan 1823
p. Trigg County Kentucky
d. 27 Nov 1892
p. Crittenden County Kentucky

15 Catherine Chisman
b.
p.
d.
p.

No. 1 on this chart is the same as no. 11 on chart no. 1

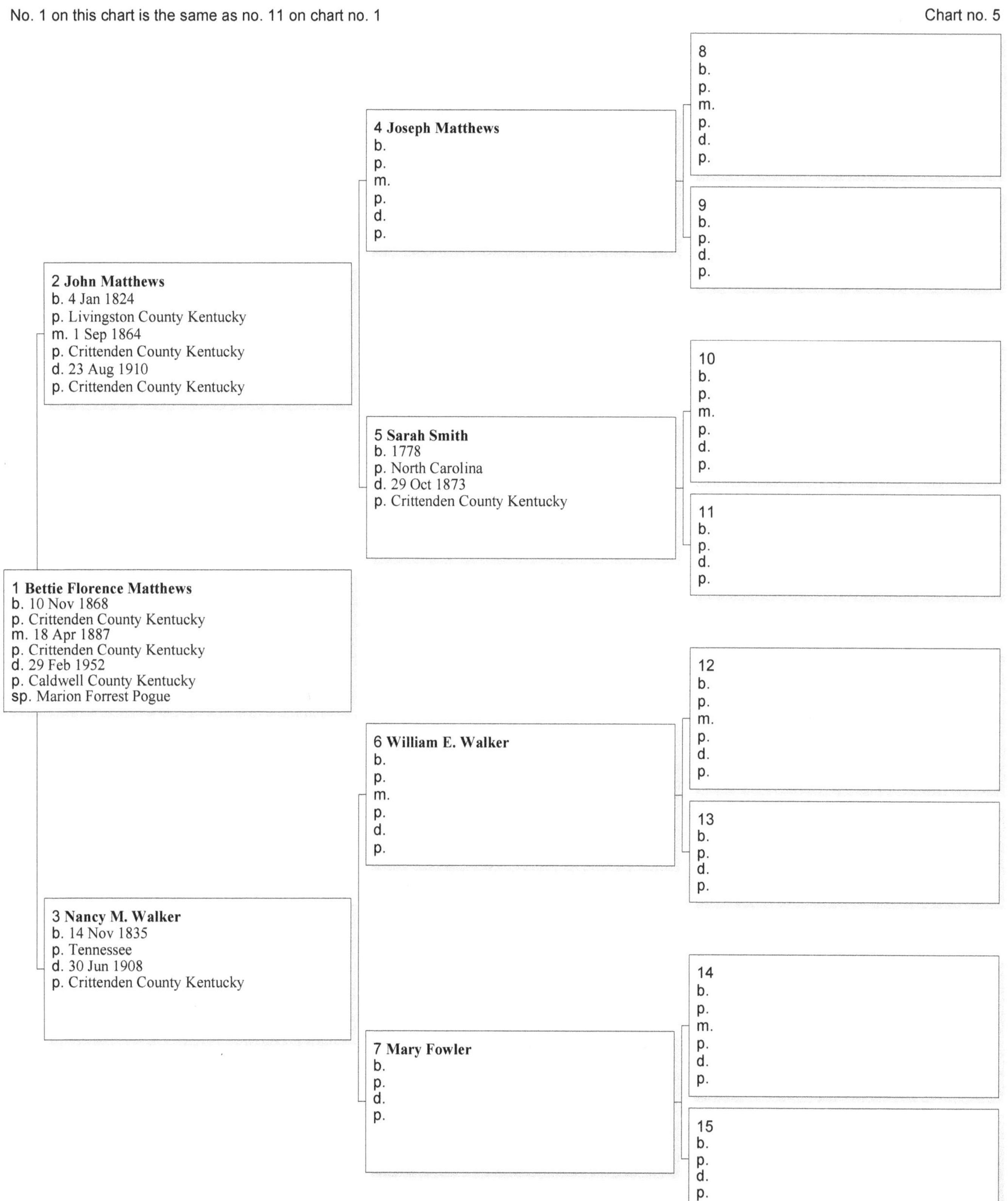

Family Tree Chart for Thomas Hubbard

No. 1 on this chart is the same as no. 12 on chart no. 1

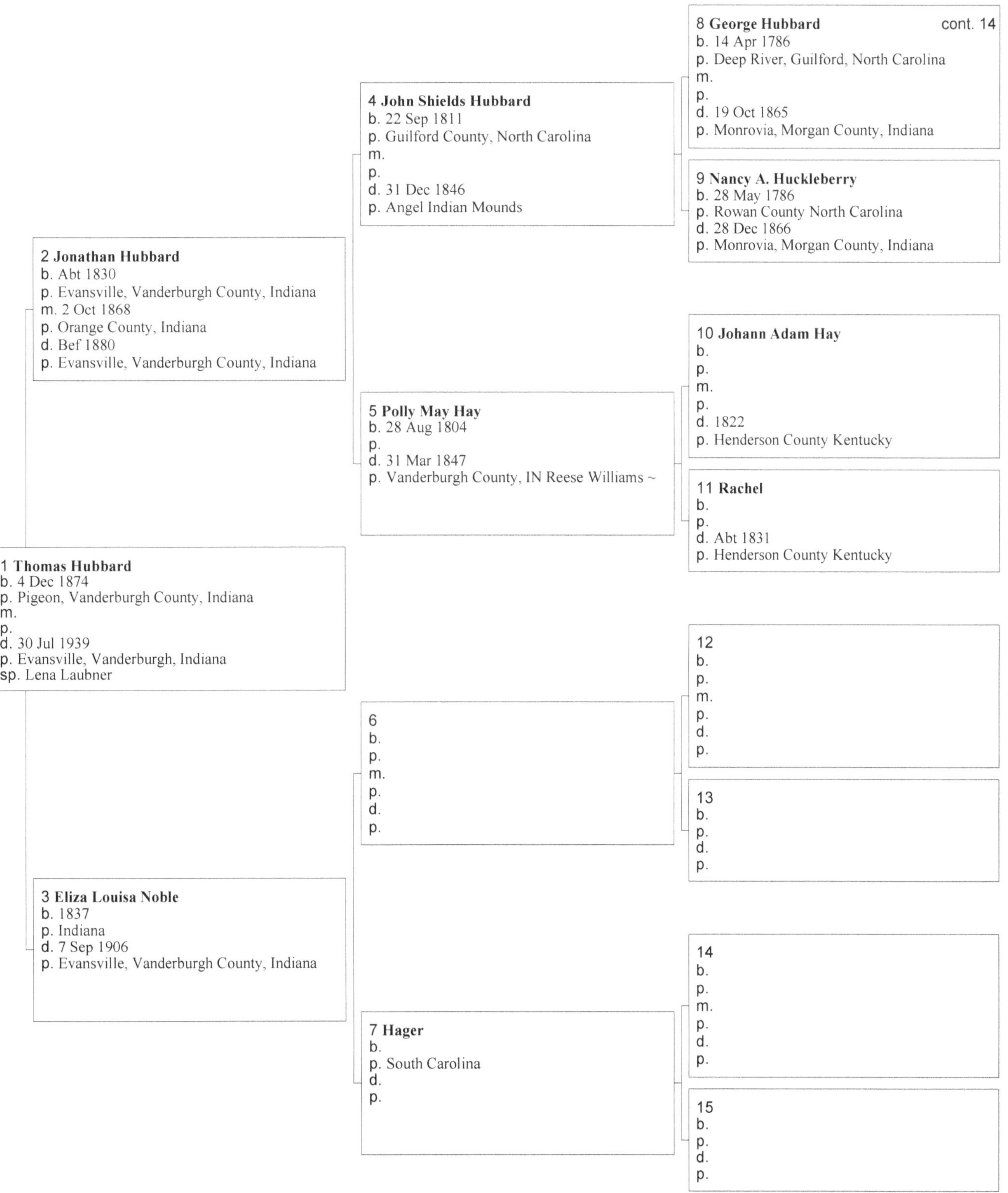

2 Jonathan Hubbard
b. Abt 1830
p. Evansville, Vanderburgh County, Indiana
m. 2 Oct 1868
p. Orange County, Indiana
d. Bef 1880
p. Evansville, Vanderburgh County, Indiana

4 John Shields Hubbard
b. 22 Sep 1811
p. Guilford County, North Carolina
m.
p.
d. 31 Dec 1846
p. Angel Indian Mounds

8 George Hubbard   cont. 14
b. 14 Apr 1786
p. Deep River, Guilford, North Carolina
m.
p.
d. 19 Oct 1865
p. Monrovia, Morgan County, Indiana

9 Nancy A. Huckleberry
b. 28 May 1786
p. Rowan County North Carolina
d. 28 Dec 1866
p. Monrovia, Morgan County, Indiana

5 Polly May Hay
b. 28 Aug 1804
p.
d. 31 Mar 1847
p. Vanderburgh County, IN Reese Williams ~

10 Johann Adam Hay
b.
p.
m.
p.
d. 1822
p. Henderson County Kentucky

11 Rachel
b.
p.
d. Abt 1831
p. Henderson County Kentucky

1 Thomas Hubbard
b. 4 Dec 1874
p. Pigeon, Vanderburgh County, Indiana
m.
p.
d. 30 Jul 1939
p. Evansville, Vanderburgh, Indiana
sp. Lena Laubner

3 Eliza Louisa Noble
b. 1837
p. Indiana
d. 7 Sep 1906
p. Evansville, Vanderburgh County, Indiana

6
b.
p.
m.
p.
d.
p.

12
b.
p.
m.
p.
d.
p.

13
b.
p.
d.
p.

7 Hager
b.
p. South Carolina
d.
p.

14
b.
p.
m.
p.
d.
p.

15
b.
p.
d.
p.

Produced by:Tennessee Research Company on 7 Jun 2018

No. 1 on this chart is the same as no. 13 on chart no. 1

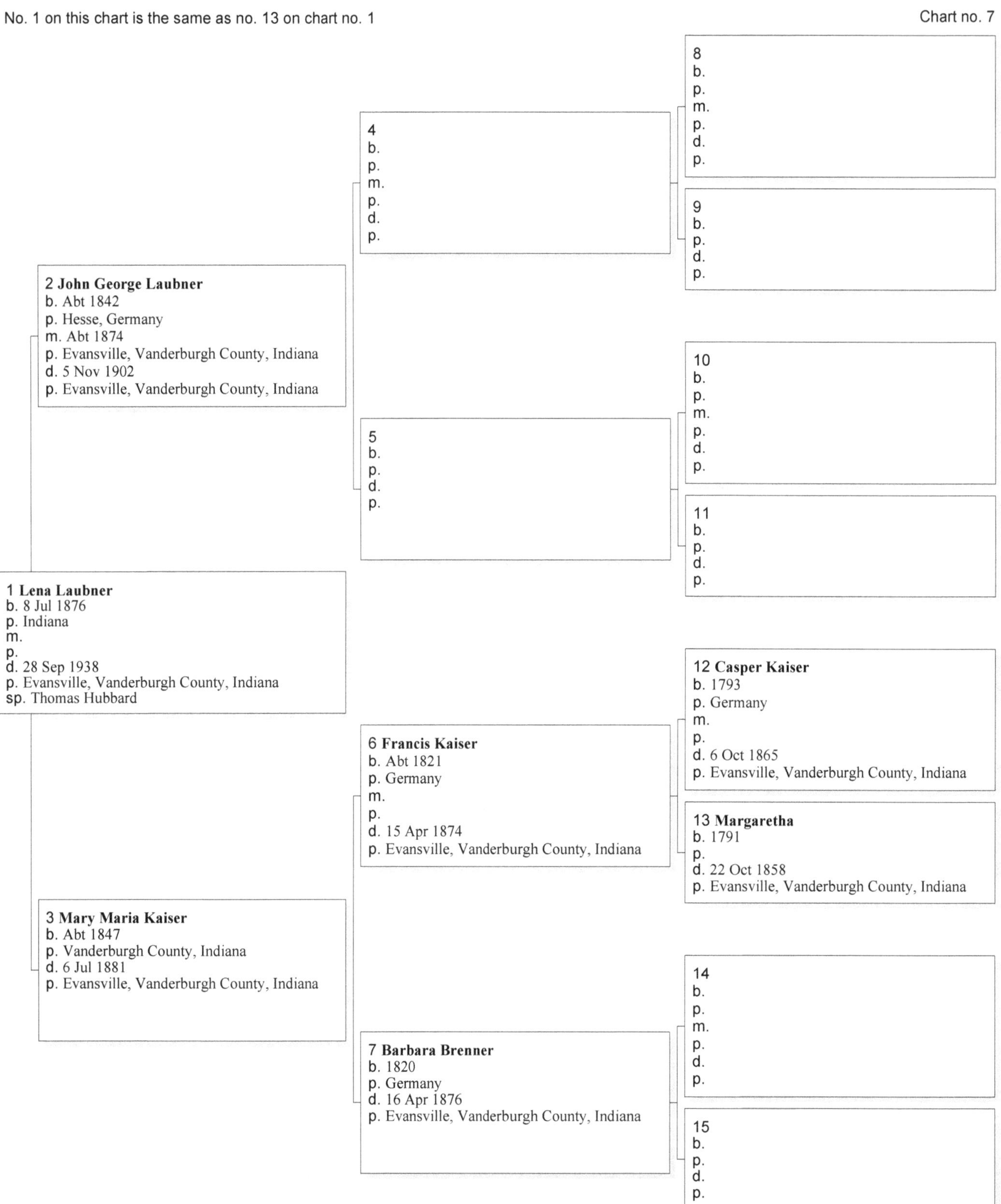

1 Lena Laubner
b. 8 Jul 1876
p. Indiana
m.
p.
d. 28 Sep 1938
p. Evansville, Vanderburgh County, Indiana
sp. Thomas Hubbard

2 John George Laubner
b. Abt 1842
p. Hesse, Germany
m. Abt 1874
p. Evansville, Vanderburgh County, Indiana
d. 5 Nov 1902
p. Evansville, Vanderburgh County, Indiana

3 Mary Maria Kaiser
b. Abt 1847
p. Vanderburgh County, Indiana
d. 6 Jul 1881
p. Evansville, Vanderburgh County, Indiana

4
b.
p.
m.
p.
d.
p.

5
b.
p.
d.
p.

6 Francis Kaiser
b. Abt 1821
p. Germany
m.
p.
d. 15 Apr 1874
p. Evansville, Vanderburgh County, Indiana

7 Barbara Brenner
b. 1820
p. Germany
d. 16 Apr 1876
p. Evansville, Vanderburgh County, Indiana

8
b.
p.
m.
p.
d.
p.

9
b.
p.
d.
p.

10
b.
p.
m.
p.
d.
p.

11
b.
p.
d.
p.

12 Casper Kaiser
b. 1793
p. Germany
m.
p.
d. 6 Oct 1865
p. Evansville, Vanderburgh County, Indiana

13 Margaretha
b. 1791
p.
d. 22 Oct 1858
p. Evansville, Vanderburgh County, Indiana

14
b.
p.
m.
p.
d.
p.

15
b.
p.
d.
p.

Family Tree Chart for Jacob Wagner

No. 1 on this chart is the same as no. 14 on chart no. 1

Family Tree Chart for Julia M. Pfingston

No. 1 on this chart is the same as no. 15 on chart no. 1

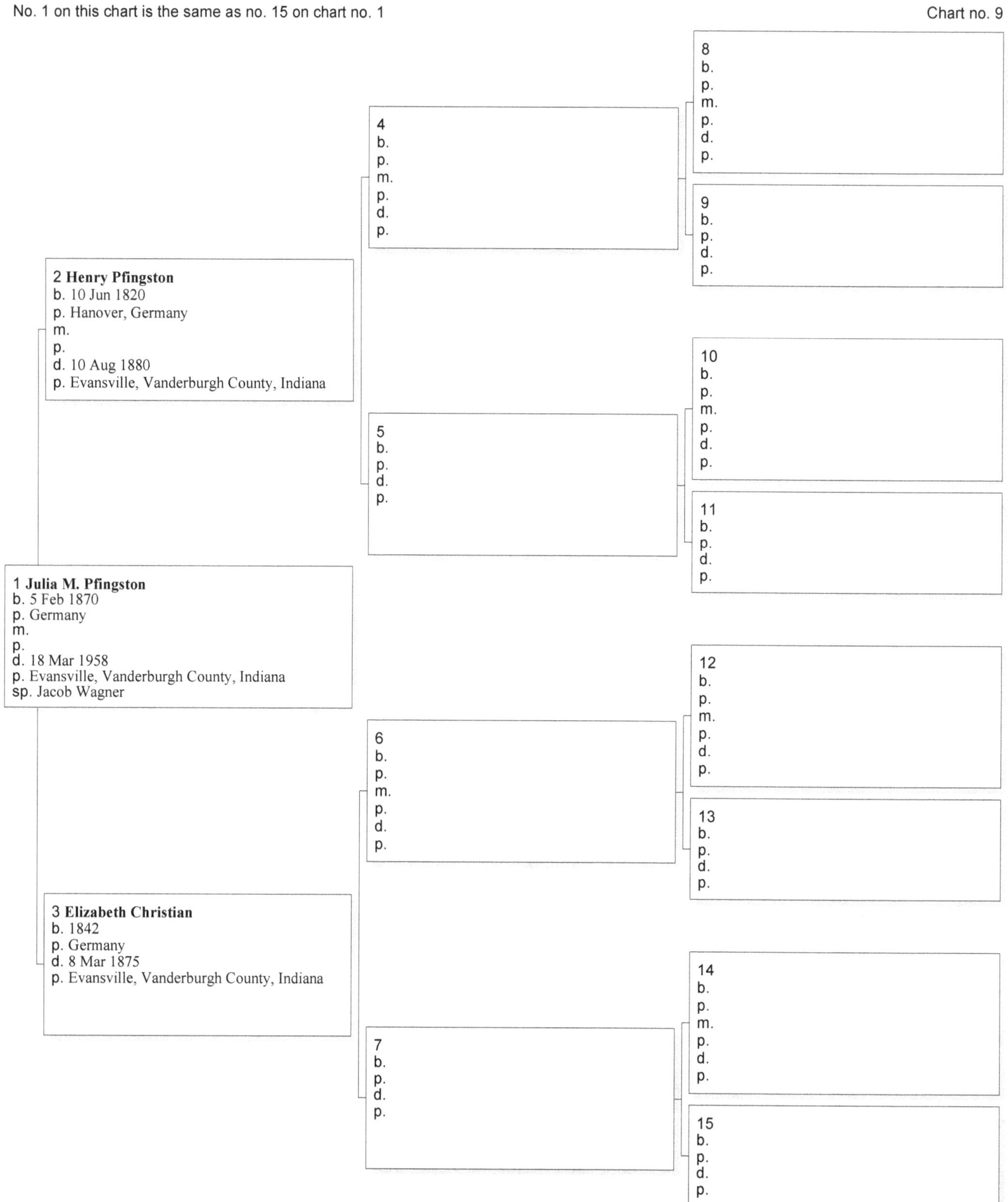

2 Henry Pfingston
b. 10 Jun 1820
p. Hanover, Germany
m.
p.
d. 10 Aug 1880
p. Evansville, Vanderburgh County, Indiana

1 Julia M. Pfingston
b. 5 Feb 1870
p. Germany
m.
p.
d. 18 Mar 1958
p. Evansville, Vanderburgh County, Indiana
sp. Jacob Wagner

3 Elizabeth Christian
b. 1842
p. Germany
d. 8 Mar 1875
p. Evansville, Vanderburgh County, Indiana

4
b.
p.
m.
p.
d.
p.

5
b.
p.
d.
p.

6
b.
p.
m.
p.
d.
p.

7
b.
p.
d.
p.

8
b.
p.
m.
p.
d.
p.

9
b.
p.
d.
p.

10
b.
p.
m.
p.
d.
p.

11
b.
p.
d.
p.

12
b.
p.
m.
p.
d.
p.

13
b.
p.
d.
p.

14
b.
p.
m.
p.
d.
p.

15
b.
p.
d.
p.

Family Tree Chart for Thomas Fox

No. 1 on this chart is the same as no. 8 on chart no. 2

8 Thomas Fox   cont. 15
b. 1593
p. Yorkshire England
m.
p.
d. 5 Nov 1624
p. Yorkshire England

4 Thomas Fox
b. Abt 1618
p. Allhallowes in Northstret, Yorkshire Engl~
m. 8 Aug 1658
p. St. Michaels in Yorkshire
d. Abt 1680
p. Yorkshire England

9
b.
p.
d.
p.

2 William Fox
b. Abt 1679
p. Yorkshire, England
m.
p.
d. 25 Dec 1741
p. Doncaster, Yorkshire, England

10
b.
p.
m.
p.
d.
p.

5 Elizabeth Renneson
b. Abt 1625
p. Bellfriraies, Yorkshire England
d.
p.

11
b.
p.
d.
p.

1 Thomas Fox
b. Abt 1739
p. Doncaster, Yorkshire, England
m. 14 Jun 1767
p. Yorkshire, England
d. 19 Sep 1801
p. Finningley, Yorkshire, England
sp. Sarah Walker

12
b.
p.
m.
p.
d.
p.

6 Bryan Shepherd
b.
p.
m. 8 Jun 1697
p. Barnsley, Yorkshire, England
d.
p.

13
b.
p.
d.
p.

3 Hannah Ann Shepherd
b. 1698
p. Barnsley, St Mary, Yorkshire, England
d.
p.

14
b.
p.
m.
p.
d.
p.

7 Elizabeth Becket
b.
p.
d.
p.

15
b.
p.
d.
p.

Family Tree Chart for Sarah Walker

No. 1 on this chart is the same as no. 9 on chart no. 2

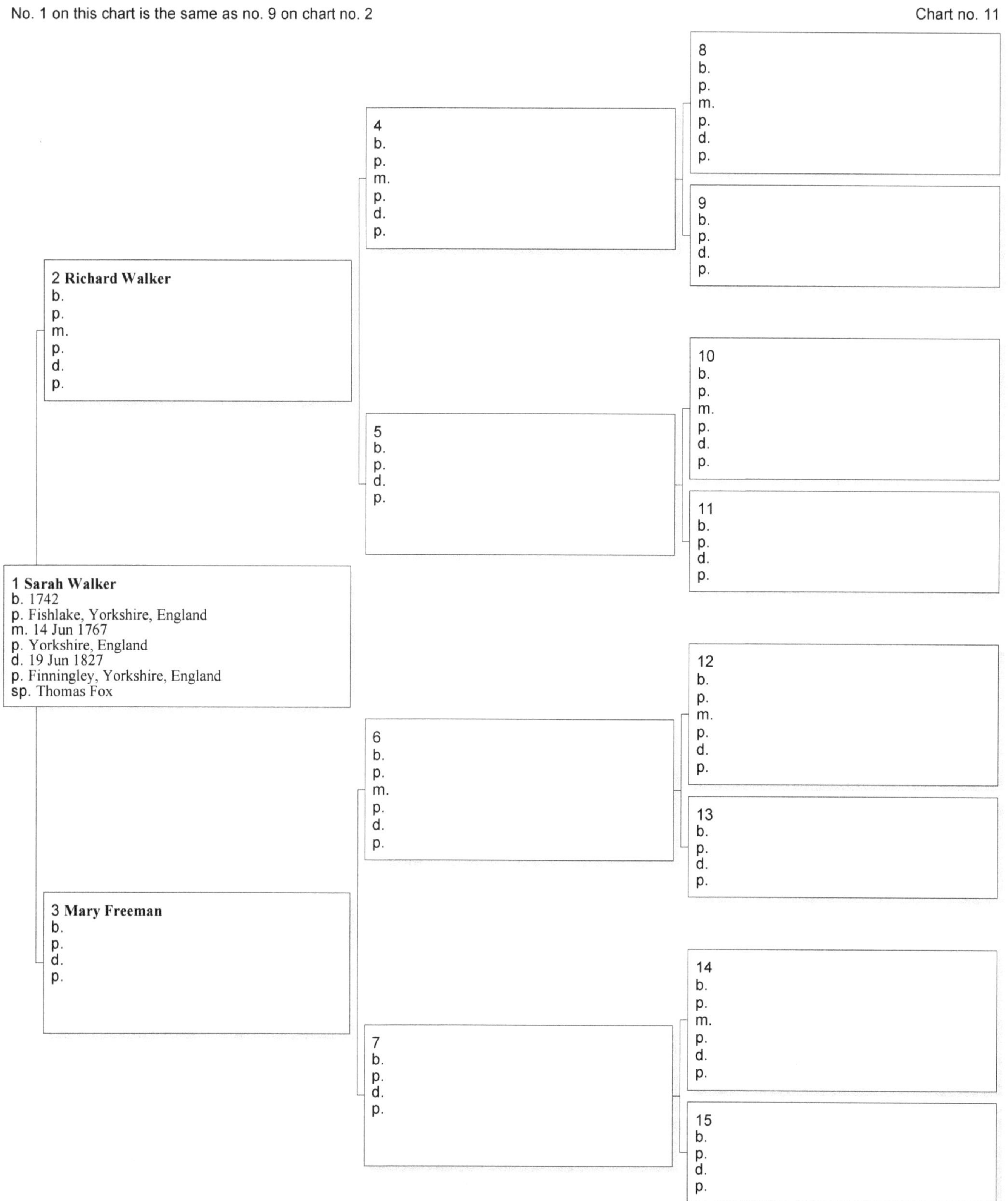

Family Tree Chart for Henry Harry Hodge

No. 1 on this chart is the same as no. 8 on chart no. 3

8 Thomas Hodge   cont. 16
b. 15 Sep 1671
p. Anna Arundel County, Maryland
m. Abt 1696
p. Anna Arundel County, Maryland
d. Abt 1731
p. Anna Arundel County, Maryland

9 Charity Ramsey
b. Abt 1684
p. Anna Arundel County, Maryland
d. Abt 1714
p. Anna Arundel County, Maryland

4 Thomas Hodge
b. 3 Nov 1697
p. Anne Arundel County, Maryland
m. Abt 1705
p. Virginia
d. Abt 1731
p. Goochland County , Virginia

2 John or Johnson Hodge
b. 1709
p. Cumberland County Virginia
m.
p.
d. 1773
p. Augusta County, Virginia

5 Christian Woodson
b. 1681
p. Cumberland County Virginia
d. Abt 1713
p. Goochland County, Virginia

10
b.
p.
m.
p.
d.
p.

11
b.
p.
d.
p.

1 Henry Harry Hodge
b. Abt 1745
p. North Carolina
m. Bef 1777
p.
d. 10 Feb 1824
p. Livingston County Kentucky
sp. Catherine Bryant

6
b.
p.
m.
p.
d.
p.

12
b.
p.
m.
p.
d.
p.

13
b.
p.
d.
p.

3 Mary
b.
p.
d.
p.

7
b.
p.
d.
p.

14
b.
p.
m.
p.
d.
p.

15
b.
p.
d.
p.

Family Tree Chart for William Thomas Pogue

No. 1 on this chart is the same as no. 8 on chart no. 4

Chart no. 13

8 Robert Pogue (Poage)
b. Abt 1699
p. Ireland
m. Abt 1722
p. Ireland
d. Abt 1732
p. Augusta County, Virginia

9 Elizabeth Preston
b.
p.
d.
p.

4 John Pogue (Poage)
b. Abt 1726
p. Ireland
m. 3 Jun 1751
p. Augusta County, Virginia
d. Abt 1789
p. Augusta County, Virginia

2 Col. William Pogue (Poage)
b. 17 Feb 1756
p. Augusta County, Virginia
m.
p.
d. 7 Apr 1830
p. Pocahontas County Virginia now West Vir~

10
b.
p.
m.
p.
d.
p.

5 Mary Blair Crawford
b. Abt 1725
p. Drumore Township, Lancaster, Pennsylvan~
d. Aft 1789
p. Augusta County, Virginia

11
b.
p.
d.
p.

1 William Thomas Pogue
b. 8 Feb 1783
p. Pocahontas County Virginia now West Virginia
m.
p.
d. 27 May 1827
p. Tazwell County Virginia
sp. Mary

12
b.
p.
m.
p.
d.
p.

6
b.
p.
m.
p.
d.
p.

13
b.
p.
d.
p.

3 Margaret Davies
b. 1749
p. Augusta County Virginia
d. 1843
p. Pocahontas County Virginia now West Vir~

14
b.
p.
m.
p.
d.
p.

7
b.
p.
d.
p.

15
b.
p.
d.
p.

Produced by:Tennessee Research Company on 7 Jun 2018

No. 1 on this chart is the same as no. 8 on chart no. 6

Chart no. 14

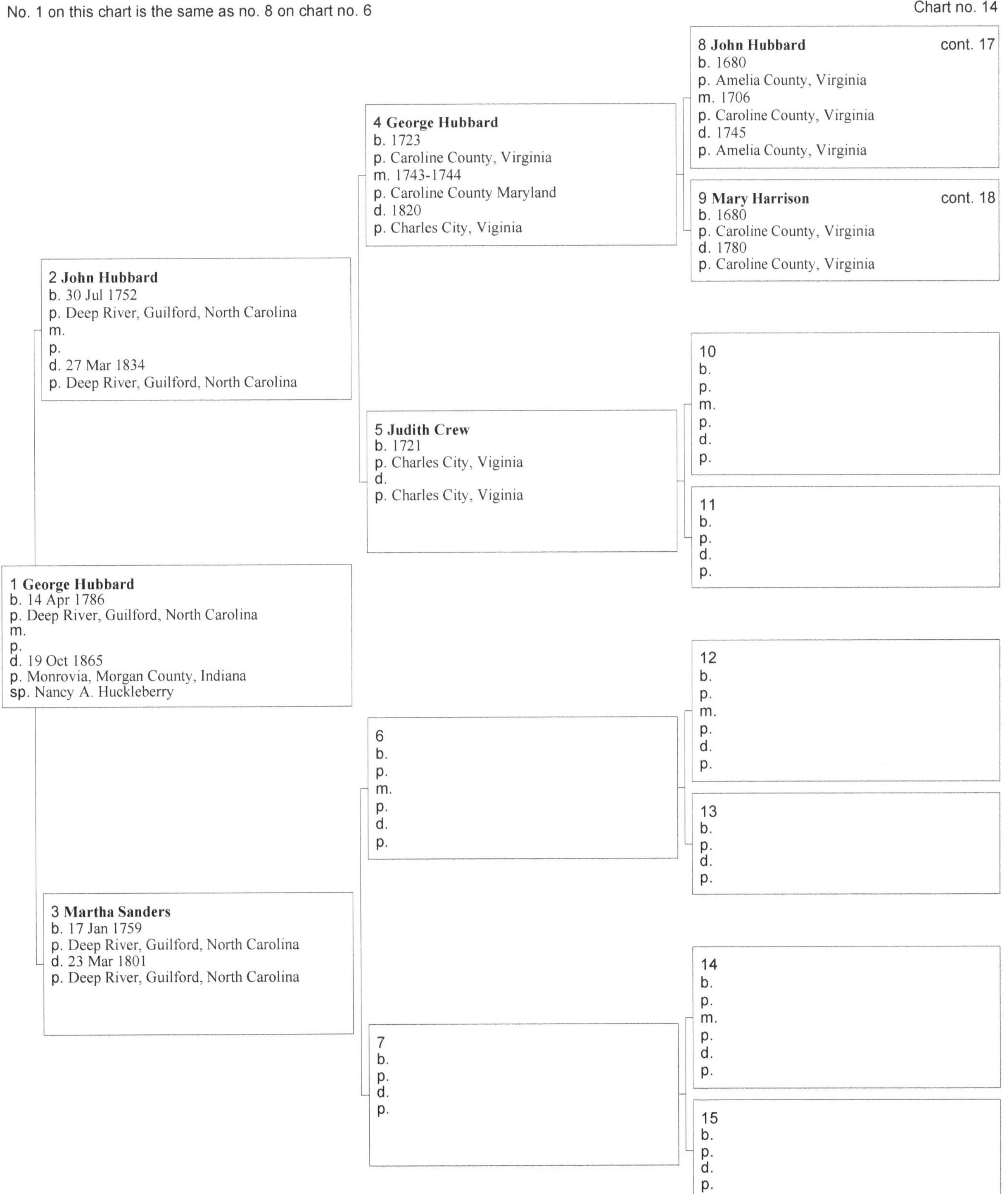

Family Tree Chart for Thomas Fox

No. 1 on this chart is the same as no. 8 on chart no. 10

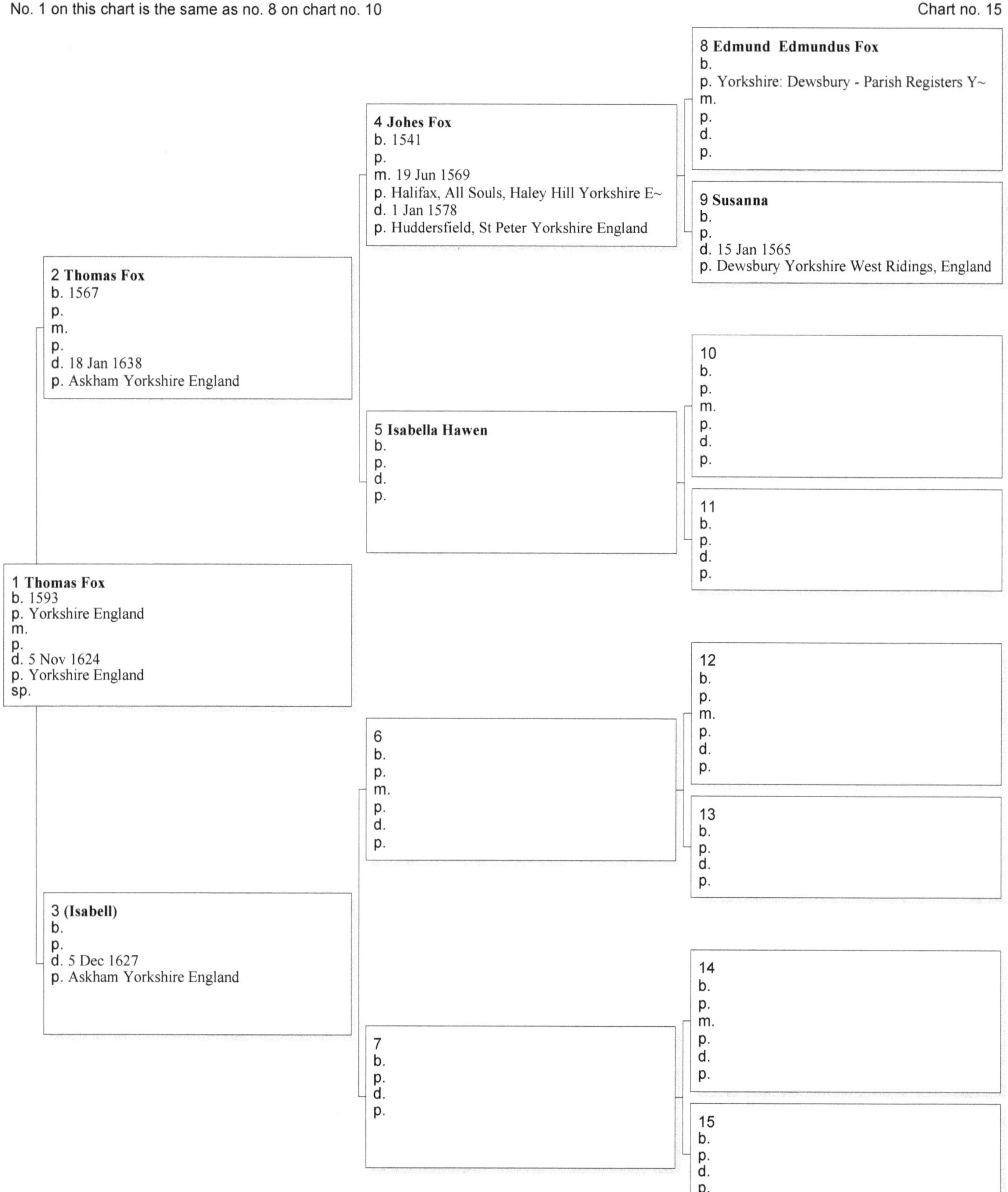

Family Tree Chart for Thomas Hodge

No. 1 on this chart is the same as no. 8 on chart no. 12

8 Humphrey Twigg Hodge
b. 1584
p. Derbyshire, England
m. 12 May 1604
p. Youlgreave, Derbyshire, England
d. 28 Feb 1624
p. Derbyshire, England

9 Margaret Timperly
b. 1584
p. Ashbourne, Derbyshire, England
d. 28 Feb 1624
p. Youlgreave, Derbyshire, England

4 Captain John Twigg Hodge
b. 1600
p. Wapping, Middlesex, England
m. Abt 1617
p. Middlesex County Massachusetts
d. 10 Oct 1654
p. Charlestown, Suffolk County, Massachusetts

5 Mary Miller
b. 1605
p. Charlestown, Middlesex County, Massach~
d. 11 Mar 1693
p. Boston Suffolk County Massachusetts

2 Humphrey Hodge
b. Abt 1623
p. Charlestown, Middlesex County, Massach~
m. Abt 1663
p. Middlesex County Mass
d. 1680
p. Barbados

1 Thomas Hodge
b. 15 Sep 1671
p. Anna Arundel County, Maryland
m. Abt 1696
p. Anna Arundel County, Maryland
d. Abt 1731
p. Anna Arundel County, Maryland
sp. Charity Ramsey

3 Mary Anderson
b. Abt 1638
p. Middlesex County Mass
d.
p.

10
b.
p.
m.
p.
d.
p.

11
b.
p.
d.
p.

6
b.
p.
m.
p.
d.
p.

7
b.
p.
d.
p.

12
b.
p.
m.
p.
d.
p.

13
b.
p.
d.
p.

14
b.
p.
m.
p.
d.
p.

15
b.
p.
d.
p.

Family Tree Chart for John Hubbard

No. 1 on this chart is the same as no. 8 on chart no. 14

8 Robert Hubbard
b. 1600
p. London, Middlesex, , England
m. 1626
p. England
d. 9 Feb 1663
p. James City, Virginia

9 Margaret Kevell
b. 1606
p. East London, England
d. 1644
p. England

4 Matthew Hubbard
b. 1627
p. Skimino, York, Virginia
m. 1661
p. Williamsburg, James, Virginia
d. 24 Apr 1667
p. York County, Virginia

2 John Hubbard
b. 1661
p. York County Virginia
m. 1675
p.
d. 1726
p. New Kent County Virginia

10
b.
p.
m.
p.
d.
p.

11
b.
p.
d.
p.

5 Sibella Caynehoe
b. 1631
p. England
d. 1665
p. York County, Virginia

1 John Hubbard
b. 1680
p. Amelia County, Virginia
m. 1706
p. Caroline County, Virginia
d. 1745
p. Amelia County, Virginia
sp. Mary Harrison

12
b.
p.
m.
p.
d.
p.

13
b.
p.
d.
p.

6
b.
p.
m.
p.
d.
p.

3 Elizabeth
b. 1663
p. Virginia
d. 1690
p. New Kent County Virginia

14
b.
p.
m.
p.
d.
p.

15
b.
p.
d.
p.

7
b.
p.
d.
p.

Family Tree Chart for Mary Harrison

No. 1 on this chart is the same as no. 9 on chart no. 14

Descendants of Edmund Edmundus Fox

First Generation

1. Edmund Edmundus Fox was born in Yorkshire: Dewsbury - Parish Registers Yorkshire England.

Edmund married **Susanna**. Susanna died on 15 Jan 1565 in Dewsbury Yorkshire West Ridings, England and was buried in St John the Baptist, Yorkshire, England.

Children from this marriage were:

+ 2 M   i.   **Johes Fox** was born in 1541, was christened on 4 Dec 1541 in Kirkburton, All Hallows Yorkshire England, and died on 1 Jan 1578 in Huddersfield, St Peter Yorkshire England at age 37.

  3 M   ii. **Edmundus Fox** died on 14 Oct 1577 in Halifax, All Souls, Haley Hill Yorkshire England.

  4 F   iii. **Johanna Fox** was born in 1548.

Second Generation (Children)

2. Johes Fox *(Edmund Edmundus [1])* was born in 1541, was christened on 4 Dec 1541 in Kirkburton, All Hallows Yorkshire England, and died on 1 Jan 1578 in Huddersfield, St Peter Yorkshire England at age 37.

Johes married **Isabella Hawen** on 19 Jun 1569 in Halifax, All Souls, Haley Hill Yorkshire England.

   Marriage Notes: She may be a secod wife

The child from this marriage was:

+ 5 M   i.   **Thomas Fox** was born in 1567, was christened on 2 Jan 1568 in Huddersfield, St Peter, and died on 18 Jan 1638 in Askham Yorkshire England at age 71.

Third Generation (Grandchildren)

5. Thomas Fox *(Johes [2], Edmund Edmundus [1])* was born in 1567, was christened on 2 Jan 1568 in Huddersfield, St Peter, and died on 18 Jan 1638 in Askham Yorkshire England at age 71.

   General Notes: Yorkshire: Allerton Mauleverer (1562-1812), Askham Richard (1578-1762 - Parish Registers (Christenings, Marriages, Burials)

Thomas married **(Isabell)**. (Isabell) died on 5 Dec 1627 in Askham Yorkshire England.

Children from this marriage were:

+ 6 M   i.   **Thomas Fox** was born in 1593 in Yorkshire England, was christened on 13 Jul 1593 in Askham Yorkshire England, and died on 5 Nov 1624 in Yorkshire England at age 31.

  7 M   ii. **Richard Fox** was born in 1597.

Fourth Generation (Great-Grandchildren)

6. Thomas Fox *(Thomas [3], Johes [2], Edmund Edmundus [1])* was born in 1593 in Yorkshire England, was christened on 13 Jul 1593 in Askham Yorkshire England, and died on 5 Nov 1624 in Yorkshire England at age 31.

Thomas married someone.

His children were:

+ 8 M   i.   **Thomas Fox** was born about 1618 in Allhallowes in Northstret, Yorkshire England and died about 1680 in Yorkshire England about age 62.

  9 M   ii. **Jonathan Fox** was born about 1620 in Yorkshire England.

 10 M   iii. **John Fox** was born about 1622.

Fifth Generation (Great Great-Grandchildren)

8. Thomas Fox *(Thomas [4], Thomas [3], Johes [2], Edmund Edmundus [1])* was born about 1618 in Allhallowes in Northstret, Yorkshire

England and died about 1680 in Yorkshire England about age 62.

General Notes: From Doncaster Parish Ye Tms Fox died 1680

Thomas married **Elizabeth Renneson** on 8 Aug 1658 in St. Michaels in Yorkshire. Elizabeth was born about 1625 in Bellfriraies, Yorkshire England.

The child from this marriage was:

+ 11   M   i.   **William Fox** was born about 1679 in Yorkshire, England and died on 25 Dec 1741 in Doncaster, Yorkshire, England about age 62.

Sixth Generation (3rd Great-Grandchildren)

11. William Fox *(Thomas [5], Thomas [4], Thomas [3], Johes [2], Edmund Edmundus [1])* was born about 1679 in Yorkshire, England and died on 25 Dec 1741 in Doncaster, Yorkshire, England about age 62.

General Notes: 1670s Britain's oldest foxhunt, the Bilsdale in Yorkshire, founded

William married **Hannah Ann Shepherd**, daughter of **Bryan Shepherd** and **Elizabeth Becket**. Hannah was born in 1698 in Barnsley, St Mary, Yorkshire, England and was christened on 1 May 1698 in Barnsley, St Mary, Yorkshire, England.

The child from this marriage was:

+ 12   M   i.   **Thomas Fox** was born about 1739 in Doncaster, Yorkshire, England, was christened on 6 May 1739 in Hatfield, Doncaster, Yorkshire, England, died on 19 Sep 1801 in Finningley, Yorkshire, England about age 62, and was buried in Holy Trinity & St. Oswald/St. Saviour.

Seventh Generation (4th Great-Grandchildren)

12. Thomas Fox *(William [6], Thomas [5], Thomas [4], Thomas [3], Johes [2], Edmund Edmundus [1])* was born about 1739 in Doncaster, Yorkshire, England, was christened on 6 May 1739 in Hatfield, Doncaster, Yorkshire, England, died on 19 Sep 1801 in Finningley, Yorkshire, England about age 62, and was buried in Holy Trinity & St. Oswald/St. Saviour.

Thomas married **Sarah Walker,** daughter of **Richard Walker** and **Mary Freeman,** on 14 Jun 1767 in Yorkshire, England. Sarah was born in 1742 in Fishlake, Yorkshire, England, was christened on 28 Dec 1742 in Fishlake, Yorkshire, England, died on 19 Jun 1827 in Finningley, Yorkshire, England at age 85, and was buried in Holy Trinity & St. Oswald/St. Saviour.

Thomas Fox Grave

Children from this marriage were:

+ 13   M   i.   **George Fox** was born on 3 Sep 1775 in Finningly, Yorkshire, , England and died on 16 Apr 1845 in Hamilton County Ohio at age 69.

   14   M   ii.   **Richard Fox.**

   15   M   iii.   **Thomas Fox.**

   16   M   iv.   **John Fox.**

Eighth Generation (5th Great-Grandchildren)

13. George Fox *(Thomas [7], William [6], Thomas [5], Thomas [4], Thomas [3], Johes [2], Edmund Edmundus [1])* was born on 3 Sep 1775 in Finningly, Yorkshire, , England and died on 16 Apr 1845 in Hamilton County Ohio at age 69.

General Notes: Fox George, Millcreek Township 05/22/1845 Will Probated 2 Richard Fox John Fox, Richard Fox, Elisabeth Fox

Descendants of Edmund Edmundus Fox

England & Wales Christening Records, 1530-1906 about George Foxx
Name: George Foxx
Gender: Male
Birth Date: abt 1775
Christening Date: 3 Sep 1775
Christening Place: Finningley, Nottinghamshire, England
Father's Name: Thomas Foxx
Mother's name: Sarah

George married **Addy Jackson** on 14 Nov 1799 in Barnsley, Yorkshire, England. Addy was born in 1775 and died on 4 Mar 1819 in Hamilton County Ohio at age 44.

Children from this marriage were:

+ 17 M   i.   **John Wesley Fox** was born about 1815-1820 in Hamilton County Ohio and died after 1880 in Crittenden County Kentucky.

  18 M   ii.   **Richard P. Fox** was born on 17 Nov 1805 in Arksey, Yorkshire, England and died on 8 Jan 1878 in Arcola, Douglas County, Illinois at age 72.

  19 F   iii.   **Addy Jane Fox** was born in 1829 and died on 19 Mar 1889 in Cleveland, Cuyahoga County, Ohio at age 60.

Ninth Generation (6th Great-Grandchildren)

17. John Wesley Fox *(George [8], Thomas [7], William [6], Thomas [5], Thomas [4], Thomas [3], Johes [2], Edmund Edmundus [1])* was born about 1815-1820 in Hamilton County Ohio and died after 1880 in Crittenden County Kentucky.

General Notes: Fox, John W.

Union

Cavalry

17th Regiment, Kentucky Cavalry

John married **Elizabeth King** about 1842 in Hamilton County Ohio. Elizabeth was born about 1825 in Hamilton County Ohio and died before 1869 in Cincinnati, Hamilton County Ohio.

Children from this marriage were:

  20 M   i.   **William A. Fox** was born about 1843 in Hamilton County Ohio.

  21 F   ii.   **Mary J. Fox** was born about 1847 in Hamilton Cointy Ohio.

+ 22 M   iii.   **Charles Wesley Fox** was born on 9 Sep 1857 in Cincinatti, Hamilton County Ohio, died on 27 Aug 1927 in Livingston, Crittenden County, Kentucky at age 69, and was buried in Owens Cemetery.

John next married **Hannah Lawson** on 11 Mar 1869 in Hamilton County Ohio. Hannah was born on 17 Oct 1821 in Cincinnati, Hamilton County, Ohio and died on 1 Dec 1877 in Miami Hamilton County Ohio at age 56.

John next married **Ellen** about 1877 in Crittenden County Kentucky. Ellen was born about 1840 in Kentucky.

Tenth Generation (7th Great-Grandchildren)

22. Charles Wesley Fox *(John Wesley [9], George [8], Thomas [7], William [6], Thomas [5], Thomas [4], Thomas [3], Johes [2], Edmund Edmundus [1])* was born on 9 Sep 1857 in Cincinatti, Hamilton County Ohio, died on 27 Aug 1927 in Livingston, Crittenden County, Kentucky at age 69, and was buried in Owens Cemetery.

Charles married **Juliet Hodge,** daughter of **Asel Branson Hodge** and **Catharine Elizabeth Millikan,** on 8 Sep 1881 in Crittenden County, Kentucky. Juliet was born on 18 Apr 1860 in Crittenden County, Kentucky, died on 20 Apr 1925 in Crittenden County, Kentucky at age 65, and was buried in Owens Cemetery.

The child from this marriage was:

+ 23 M   i.   **Vernon Richard Fox** was born on 2 May 1884 in Lebanon, Marion County, Kentucky and died in May 1968 in Manila, Mississippi County Arkansas at age 84.

Descendants of Edmund Edmundus Fox

11th Generation (8th Great-Grandchildren)

23. Vernon Richard Fox *(Charles Wesley [10], John Wesley [9], George [8], Thomas [7], William [6], Thomas [5], Thomas [4], Thomas [3], Johes [2], Edmund Edmundus [1])* was born on 2 May 1884 in Lebanon, Marion County, Kentucky and died in May 1968 in Manila, Mississippi County Arkansas at age 84.

Vernon married **Clara Augusta Pogue,** daughter of **Marion Forrest Pogue** and **Bettie Florence Matthews,** in 1909 in Crittenden County Kentucky. Clara was born on 12 May 1888 in Crittenden County Kentucky and died in Aug 1936 in Manila, Mississippi County Arkansas at age 48.

Noted events in her life were:
• Cause of Death: colon cancer.

Children from this marriage were:

24 F i. **Thelma N. Fox** was born on 16 Feb 1911 in Crittenden County Kentucky and died in 1919 in Maniila, Mississippi County Arkansas at age 8.

+ 25 F ii. **Marian Verna Fox** was born on 18 Dec 1913 in Crittenden County Kentucky, died on 25 Jul 1999 in Greeley, Weld County, Colorado at age 85, and was buried in Manila Cemetery.

26 M iii. **Richard Wesley Fox** was born on 26 May 1916 in Manila, Mississippi County Arkansas and died on 11 May 2006 in Traverse City, MI at age 89. The cause of his death was Demintia and Stroke.

+ 27 M iv. **William Garrad Fox** was born on 21 Aug 1918 in Manila, Mississippi County, Arkansas, died on 14 Nov 2007 in Lenoir City, Loudon County, Tennessee at age 89, and was buried in Manila Cemetery.

12th Generation (9th Great-Grandchildren)

25. Marian Verna Fox *(Vernon Richard [11], Charles Wesley [10], John Wesley [9], George [8], Thomas [7], William [6], Thomas [5], Thomas [4], Thomas [3], Johes [2], Edmund Edmundus [1])* was born on 18 Dec 1913 in Crittenden County Kentucky, died on 25 Jul 1999 in Greeley, Weld County, Colorado at age 85, and was buried in Manila Cemetery.

Marian married **James Nelson Moore**, son of **George Nelson Moore** and **Ida May Billings**. James was born on 19 Nov 1913 in Manila, Mississippi County Arkansas, died on 27 Nov 1962 in Memphis, Shelby County Tennessee at age 49, and was buried in Manila Cemetery.

Children from this marriage were:

28 M i. **James Nelson Moore Jr** was born on 26 Nov 1933 in Manila, Mississippi County Arkansas and died on 23 Sep 1983 in Denver Colorado at age 49.

29 M ii. **Robert Garrad Moore** was born on 23 Feb 1937 in Manila, Mississippi County Arkansas.

Robert married **Virginia Ann Johnson,** daughter of **Uriel Lee Johnson** and **Charlene Montine McMahan,** on 17 Jul 1959 in Little Rock, Pulaski County, Arkansas. Virginia was born on 12 Feb 1941 in Little Rock, Pulaski County, Arkansas.

30 M iii. **Richard Marion Moore** was born on 23 Feb 1937 in Manila, Mississippi County Arkansas.

+ 31 F iv. **Brenda Kathryn Moore** was born on 6 Sep 1941 in Blytheville, Mississippi County, Arkansas.

Marian next married **Robert Joseph Wambaugh**. Robert was born on 28 Feb 1929 in Pennsylvania and died on 15 Sep 1999 in Greeley, Weld County, Colorado at age 70.

27. William Garrad Fox *(Vernon Richard [11], Charles Wesley [10], John Wesley [9], George [8], Thomas [7], William [6], Thomas [5], Thomas [4], Thomas [3], Johes [2], Edmund Edmundus [1])* was born on 21 Aug 1918 in Manila, Mississippi County, Arkansas, died on 14 Nov 2007 in Lenoir City, Loudon County, Tennessee at age 89, and was buried in Manila Cemetery.

Descendants of Edmund Edmundus Fox

William married **Marion Francis Hubbard,** daughter of **Marvin Dean Hubbard** and **Lydia Wagner,** on 20 Feb 1943 in Detroit, Wayne, Michigan. Marion was born on 17 Dec 1923 in Evansville, Vanderburgh County, Indiana, died on 3 Mar 2012 in Lenoir City Loudon County Tennessee at age 88, and was buried in Manila Cemetery.

Children from this marriage were:

    32 M   i. **Gary Fox**.

               Gary married **Barbara Jean Sinclair**, daughter of **George Taylor Sinclair** and **Betty Lou Grooms**.

    33 M   ii. **Rick Fox**.

13th Generation (10th Great-Grandchildren)

31. Brenda Kathryn Moore *(Marian Verna Fox [12], Vernon Richard [11], Charles Wesley [10], John Wesley [9], George [8], Thomas [7], William [6], Thomas [5], Thomas [4], Thomas [3], Johes [2], Edmund Edmundus [1])* was born on 6 Sep 1941 in Blytheville, Mississippi County, Arkansas.

Brenda married **Walter Bradsher Mewborn,** son of **William Gordon Mewborn** and **Eula Elizabeth Bradsher,** on 25 Dec 1960 in Somerville, Fayette County, Tennessee. Walter was born on 19 Nov 1939 in Shelby County Tennessee, died on 4 Nov 2008 in Fayette County Tennessee at age 68, and was buried in Fayette County Memorial Park.

Children from this marriage were:

 + 34 F   i. **Melinda Lyn Mewborn** was born on 29 Jan 1962 in Knoxville, Knox County Tennessee.

 + 35 F   ii. **Terri Ann Mewborn** was born on 20 Jun 1963 in Knoxville, Knox County Tennessee.

14th Generation (11th Great-Grandchildren)

34. Melinda Lyn Mewborn *(Brenda Kathryn Moore [13], Marian Verna Fox [12], Vernon Richard [11], Charles Wesley [10], John Wesley [9], George [8], Thomas [7], William [6], Thomas [5], Thomas [4], Thomas [3], Johes [2], Edmund Edmundus [1])* was born on 29 Jan 1962 in Knoxville, Knox County Tennessee.

Melinda married **Robert Michael Franklin** on 27 Aug 1982 in Memphis, Shelby County Tennessee. Robert was born on 23 Jan 1958 in Memphis, Shelby County Tennessee.

The child from this marriage was:

    36 F   i. **Leah Michelle Franklin** was born on 20 May 2002 in Memphis, Shelby County Tennessee.

35. Terri Ann Mewborn *(Brenda Kathryn Moore [13], Marian Verna Fox [12], Vernon Richard [11], Charles Wesley [10], John Wesley [9], George [8], Thomas [7], William [6], Thomas [5], Thomas [4], Thomas [3], Johes [2], Edmund Edmundus [1])* was born on 20 Jun 1963 in Knoxville, Knox County Tennessee.

Terri married **Alpheus Robert Kelley II** on 4 Dec 1982 in Memphis, Shelby County Tennessee. Alpheus was born on 28 Apr 1958.

Children from this marriage were:

    37 F   i. **Kristen Leigh Kelley** was born on 11 May 1986 in Memphis, Shelby County Tennessee.

    38 F   ii. **Katelyn Ann Kelley** was born on 6 Sep 1989 in Memphis, Shelby County Tennessee.

Terri next married **Robert Cephus White** on 14 May 1994. Robert was born on 7 May 1956.

First Generation

39. Humphrey Twigg Hodge was born in 1584 in Derbyshire, England and died on 28 Feb 1624 in Derbyshire, England at age 40.

Humphrey married **Margaret Timperly** on 12 May 1604 in Youlgreave, Derbyshire, England. Margaret was born in 1584 in Ashbourne, Derbyshire, England and died on 28 Feb 1624 in Youlgreave, Derbyshire, England at age 40.

The child from this marriage was:

+ 40 M   i.   **Captain John Twigg Hodge** was born in 1600 in Wapping, Middlesex, England and died on 10 Oct 1654 in Charlestown, Suffolk County, Massachusetts at age 54.

Second Generation (Children)

40. Captain John Twigg Hodge *(Humphrey Twigg [1])* was born in 1600 in Wapping, Middlesex, England and died on 10 Oct 1654 in Charlestown, Suffolk County, Massachusetts at age 54.

> General Notes: In November, 1633, the Rebecca, of about 60 tons, was built at Medford, Mass., for Gov. Matthew Cradock and his partners, and William Pierce was given command. Perhaps John Hodges was mate. We know that on Dec. 18, 1634, the Rebecca, Capt. William Pierce, sailed from Massachusetts for England; and on April 6 and 9, 1635, the Rebecca, Capt. John Hodges, was at London taking passengers and freight for New England. In 1635 and 1636 John Hodges was making constant trips in the Rebecca, plying between Boston and Connecticut, with letters and commissions of Gov. John Winthrop, senior, of Massachusetts and Gov. John Winthrop, junior, of Connecticut, going north to the Isle of Sable for sea-horse and cows, and south to Bermuda, whence he returned with "30,000 weight of potatoes and store of oranges and limes." Early in 1637 Matthew Cradock in London wrote to Gov. Winthrop in Boston, directing that John Hodges should resume command of the Rebecca and take this ship with her "ordnance," and victualled for three months, to Virginia. Why "resume" is not stated, nor whether John Hodges and the Rebecca made this voyage.

> kathilieoriginally submitted this to Hodges-Boles-Gruggett-Flores on 11 Sep 2009

John married **Mary Miller** about 1617 in Middlesex County Massachusetts. Mary was born in 1605 in Charlestown, Middlesex County, Massachusetts and died on 11 Mar 1693 in Boston Suffolk County Massachusetts at age 88.

The child from this marriage was:

+ 41 M   i.   **Humphrey Hodge** was born about 1623 in Charlestown, Middlesex County, Massachusetts and died in 1680 in Barbados about age 57.

Third Generation (Grandchildren)

41. Humphrey Hodge *(John Twigg (Captain) [2], Humphrey Twigg [1])* was born about 1623 in Charlestown, Middlesex County, Massachusetts and died in 1680 in Barbados about age 57.

> General Notes: Persecution as Quaker

> The first meeting of Friends in Boston, of which we have account, was at the house of Mr. Wanton, on the 4th of May, when a warrant was issued to apprehend the preacher, and report the names of his hearers to the governour. The spirit of persecution was kept alive and manifested itself in various ways, after this. On the 9ih of August, l675, there were dQuakers apprehended, at their ordinary place of meeting, Kobt. Edmund, Edw. Shippen, John Soames, Jere. Debee, Geo. Danson, Miles Foster, Humphrey Hodges, Bridget Phillips, Thos. Scott, Wm. Nrlal, Eph. Stratton, Elizabeth Bowers (senior and junior), Geo. Walker. Twelve of these 14 were whipped ; the other two paid their fines.

> from A History of Boston: The Metropolis of Massachusetts by Caleb Hopkins Snow - 1828 - Boston (Mass.)

Humphrey married **Mary Anderson** about 1663 in Middlesex County Mass. Mary was born about 1638 in Middlesex County Mass.

The child from this marriage was:

+ 42 M   i.   **Thomas Hodge** was born on 15 Sep 1671 in Anna Arundel County, Maryland and died about 1731 in Anna Arundel County, Maryland about age 60.

Fourth Generation (Great-Grandchildren)

42. Thomas Hodge *(Humphrey ³, John Twigg (Captain) ², Humphrey Twigg ¹)* was born on 15 Sep 1671 in Anna Arundel County, Maryland and died about 1731 in Anna Arundel County, Maryland about age 60.

> General Notes: Thomas Barnes, son of Humphrey and Mary, was born 15 September 1671. He arrived in Pennsylvania with his mother and stepfather on 20 August 1683. Although there are one or two Thomas Hodges appearing in the records of Philadelphia Meetings, Kenneth Hodges advances compelling reasons why the Thomaas who married Charity Ramsey may well have left the Quaker fold and become Episcopalian. On 13 May 1697 he witnessed the will of John Belt of Anne Arundel Co. Thomas disappeared from Maryland records after the death of Charity (who died before 1714).

Thomas married **Charity Ramsey** about 1696 in Anna Arundel County, Maryland. Charity was born about 1684 in Anna Arundel County, Maryland and died about 1714 in Anna Arundel County, Maryland about age 30.

The child from this marriage was:
+ 43 M   i. **Thomas Hodge** was born on 3 Nov 1697 in Anne Arundel County, Maryland and died about 1731 in Goochland County , Virginia about age 34.

Fifth Generation (Great Great-Grandchildren)

43. Thomas Hodge *(Thomas ⁴, Humphrey ³, John Twigg (Captain) ², Humphrey Twigg ¹)* was born on 3 Nov 1697 in Anne Arundel County, Maryland and died about 1731 in Goochland County , Virginia about age 34.

Thomas married **Christian Woodson** about 1705 in Virginia. Christian was born in 1681 in Cumberland County Virginia and died about 1713 in Goochland County, Virginia about age 32.

The child from this marriage was:
+ 44 M   i. **John or Johnson Hodge** was born in 1709 in Cumberland County Virginia and died in 1773 in Augusta County, Virginia at age 64.

Sixth Generation (3rd Great-Grandchildren)

44. John or Johnson Hodge *(Thomas ⁵, Thomas ⁴, Humphrey ³, John Twigg (Captain) ², Humphrey Twigg ¹)* was born in 1709 in Cumberland County Virginia and died in 1773 in Augusta County, Virginia at age 64.

> General Notes: Thomas Hodges who wrote his will in 1749 probated in 1750 in Cumberland Co., Va. (made from Goochland Co., Va.) Abstract of Thomas Hodges will names Christian (his wife) and William Womack as co-executors and makes bequests to his children William, John, Drury, Thomas, Edmund, Mary, and Delany. Witnessed by Henry Bell, John Chafin, and William Mills. An interesting tidbit is that T. Hodges also knew the Governor Richard Bennett excerpt from his will as follows   (...Lastly, I do hereby declare and ordain and appoint James Jofey, Mr. Thomas Hodges, and Edmond Belson or any two of them also Robert Pealle to be overseers of this my last will and testament allowing & approving for good and effectual to all intents and purposes what so ever my said executors or any two of them shall do or cause to be done concerning the estate from time to time in relation to the estate.) Thomas Hodges was also one of the witnesses to the marriage of Edmond Belson son of Elizabeth Belson of Nansemond Co. to Mary Crew, daughter of Mary Took of Isle of Wight Co. on 13 Nov. 1684 I Valentine Papers 210, (from the records of to Society of Friends, Lower Virginia Meeting).
>
> Edmund Hodges was next in my line. With Edmund we have a good deal of data that exists today. Edmund performed the patriotic service of furnishing supplies for the soldiers during the Revolutionary War. (Source: Hodges Notes Hart Co. Historical Society from Chatham, Va. courthouse.)
> Abstra ct of Edmund Hodges Will it reads in part:
> (...I Edmund Hodges of the County of Pittsylvania... lend to my loving wife Nephany during her natural life or widowhood my whole estate...
> ...to my five sons John Hodges, Thomas Hodges, Moses Hodges, David Hodges, and Jesse Hodges eight hundred acres of land to be divided amongst them so that my son Thomas have is land where I now dwell and my son David to have his land taking the place where Samuel Morley (Mosley sp?) did settle on and if it please God to take me out of this world before I do clear out the survey that was surveyed for me adjoining the patton (pattern?) land the money to be paid out of my estate for the clearing the land out of the office...) This will lists wife and 5 boys. And later in a codicil we find a daughter Susannah Hodges. This daughter married a John Slayden, there is some question as to exact spelling of his name, but I will use Slayden here.   (In a codicil dated 11 Feb 1782 and witnessed by Joseph Akin, William Briswell, and Robert Hopper

...My daughter Susannah Slayton's equal part of my moveabel Estate which I do hereby revoke and disannul as she has since deceased. I do will and bequeath the same part of my moveable estate which was allotted to her to be equally divided amongst her six children viz: James, Rachel, Pattsey, John, Edmund, and Arthur Porter Slayton....) Here we have what looks to be a sad event, a daughter passing on. I still haven't a clear mind on Edmund there is still some data that does not all fit. From my aunt Geraldine Hodges I have her saying Edmund was a "native of Ireland... migrating to America and settling in Virginia." The research I have does not fit exactly with this thought. Edmund although not a common name does appear in more than one place. I feel he is the Edmund of Goochland Co.This deed mentions Edmund. .Joseph Scott of Goochland Co. sold 20 A ... Lickinghole Creek to Edmund Hodges... Joseph Scott of Amelia Co. sold to Henry Wood ... 400 A on the North side of James Rive... Lickinghole Creek, excepting 20 A conveyed to Edmund Hodges. Our Edmund marry's Nephanah Walker and has 9 children. They were married in St James Northam Parish, in Goochland Co. The church in the 1700's was of great importance in people's lives. Birth's, death's, social events, everyone went to the church, they were the hub along with the town, which peoples lives were intertwined.

John married **Mary**.

The child from this marriage was:

+ 45   M   i.   **Henry Harry Hodge** was born about 1745 in North Carolina and died on 10 Feb 1824 in Livingston County Kentucky about age 79.

Seventh Generation (4th Great-Grandchildren)

45. Henry Harry Hodge *(John or Johnson [6], Thomas [5], Thomas [4], Humphrey [3], John Twigg (Captain) [2], Humphrey Twigg [1])* was born about 1745 in North Carolina and died on 10 Feb 1824 in Livingston County Kentucky about age 79.

Henry married **Catherine Bryant** before 1777. Catherine was born in 1752 in North Carolina and died about 1794 in Livingston County Kentucky about age 42.

The child from this marriage was:

+ 46   M   i.   **William Fidella Hodge** was born in 1777 in Edgecombe County North Carolina and died in 1826 in Livingston County Kentucky at age 49.

Eighth Generation (5th Great-Grandchildren)

46. William Fidella Hodge *(Henry Harry [7], John or Johnson [6], Thomas [5], Thomas [4], Humphrey [3], John Twigg (Captain) [2], Humphrey Twigg [1])* was born in 1777 in Edgecombe County North Carolina and died in 1826 in Livingston County Kentucky at age 49.

William married **Nancy Josiphine Dancy**.

The child from this marriage was:

+ 47   M   i.   **Asel Branson Hodge** was born on 18 Jan 1825 in Livingston County Kentucky and died on 4 Jan 1889 in Crittenden County Kentucky at age 63.

Ninth Generation (6th Great-Grandchildren)

47. Asel Branson Hodge *(William Fidella [8], Henry Harry [7], John or Johnson [6], Thomas [5], Thomas [4], Humphrey [3], John Twigg (Captain) [2], Humphrey Twigg [1])* was born on 18 Jan 1825 in Livingston County Kentucky and died on 4 Jan 1889 in Crittenden County Kentucky at age 63.

Asel married **Catharine Elizabeth Millikan**, daughter of **Solomon Millikan** and **Nancy Morgan**. Catharine was born on 16 Oct 1829 in Grainger County Tennessee and died on 18 Dec 1889 in Crittenden County Kentucky at age 60.

The child from this marriage was:

+ 48   F   i.   **Juliet Hodge** was born on 18 Apr 1860 in Crittenden County, Kentucky, died on 20 Apr 1925 in Crittenden County, Kentucky at age 65, and was buried in Owens Cemetery.

Tenth Generation (7th Great-Grandchildren)

48. .Juliet Hodge *(Asel Branson [9], William Fidella [8], Henry Harry [7], .John or Johnson [6], Thomas [5], Thomas [4], Humphrey [3], John Twigg (Captain) [2], Humphrey Twigg [1])* was born on 18 Apr 1860 in Crittenden County, Kentucky, died on 20 Apr 1925 in Crittenden County, Kentucky at age 65, and was buried in Owens Cemetery.

Juliet married **Charles Wesley Fox,** son of **John Wesley Fox** and **Elizabeth King,** on 8 Sep 1881 in Crittenden County, Kentucky. Charles was born on 9 Sep 1857 in Cincinatti, Hamilton County Ohio, died on 27 Aug 1927 in Livingston, Crittenden County, Kentucky at age 69, and was buried in Owens Cemetery.

(Duplicate Line. See Person 22 on Page 21)

Descendants of Robert Pogue (Poage)

First Generation

49. Robert Pogue (Poage) was born about 1699 in Ireland and died about 1732 in Augusta County, Virginia about age 33.

Robert married **Elizabeth Preston** about 1722 in Ireland.

The child from this marriage was:

+ 50 M   i. **John Pogue (Poage)** was born about 1726 in Ireland and died about 1789 in Augusta County, Virginia about age 63.

Second Generation (Children)

50. John Pogue (Poage) *(Robert [1])* was born about 1726 in Ireland and died about 1789 in Augusta County, Virginia about age 63.

John married **Mary Blair Crawford** on 3 Jun 1751 in Augusta County, Virginia. Mary was born about 1725 in Drumore Township, Lancaster, Pennsylvania, USA and died after 1789 in Augusta County, Virginia.

The child from this marriage was:

+ 51 M   i. **Col. William Pogue (Poage)** was born on 17 Feb 1756 in Augusta County, Virginia and died on 7 Apr 1830 in Pocahontas County Virginia now West Virginia at age 74.

Third Generation (Grandchildren)

51. Col. William Pogue (Poage) *(John [2], Robert [1])* was born on 17 Feb 1756 in Augusta County, Virginia and died on 7 Apr 1830 in Pocahontas County Virginia now West Virginia at age 74.

William married **Margaret Davies**. Margaret was born in 1749 in Augusta County Virginia and died in 1843 in Pocahontas County Virginia now West Virginia at age 94.

The child from this marriage was:

+ 52 M   i. **William Thomas Pogue** was born on 8 Feb 1783 in Pocahontas County Virginia now West Virginia and died on 27 May 1827 in Tazwell County Virginia at age 44.

Fourth Generation (Great-Grandchildren)

52. William Thomas Pogue *(William (Col.) [3], John [2], Robert [1])* was born on 8 Feb 1783 in Pocahontas County Virginia now West Virginia and died on 27 May 1827 in Tazwell County Virginia at age 44.

William married **Mary**. Mary was born in 1784 in Virginia.

Children from this marriage were:

+ 53 M   i. **Thomas Franklin Pogue** was born on 21 Jan 1802 in Tazwell County Virginia, died on 20 Jun 1857 in Calloway County, Kentucky at age 55, and was buried in Pogue Cemetery.

   54 M   ii. **Hiram Pogue** was born about 1814 in Virginia.

Fifth Generation (Great Great-Grandchildren)

53. Thomas Franklin Pogue *(William Thomas [4], William (Col.) [3], John [2], Robert [1])* was born on 21 Jan 1802 in Tazwell County Virginia, died on 20 Jun 1857 in Calloway County, Kentucky at age 55, and was buried in Pogue Cemetery.

     General Notes: His death Record states Sabbed he was an Outlaw

Thomas married **Harriet Cruise,** daughter of **Jonathan Cruise** and **Holly Bennett,** on 26 Dec 1844 in Graves County Kentucky. Harriet was born on 11 May 1823 in North Carolina, died on 1 Dec 1892 in Calloway County, Kentucky at age 69, and was buried in Pogue Cemetery.

The child from this marriage was:

+ 55 M   i. **William Washington Pogue** was born on 11 Dec 1845 in Murray, Calloway County, Kentucky, died on 5 Mar 1926 in Crittenden County Kentucky at age 80, and was buried in Oliver Cemetery.

Descendants of Robert Pogue (Poage)

Sixth Generation (3rd Great-Grandchildren)

55. William Washington Pogue *(Thomas Franklin [5], William Thomas [4], William (Col.) [3], John [2], Robert [1])* was born on 11 Dec 1845 in Murray, Calloway County, Kentucky, died on 5 Mar 1926 in Crittenden County Kentucky at age 80, and was buried in Oliver Cemetery.

William married **Mary Catherine Oliver,** daughter of **Henry W. Oliver** and **Margaret C. Rolston,** on 19 Dec 1866 in Crittenden County Kentucky. Mary was born on 22 Jul 1849 in Crittenden County Kentucky, died on 14 Apr 1939 in Crittenden County Kentucky at age 89, and was buried in Oliver Cemetery.

The child from this marriage was:
+ 56 M i. **Marion Forrest Pogue** was born on 18 Oct 1867 in Crittenden County Kentucky, died on 26 Sep 1952 in Caldwell County Kentucky at age 84, and was buried in Frances Presbyterian Church Cemetery Frances Crittenden County Kentucky.

Seventh Generation (4th Great-Grandchildren)

56. Marion Forrest Pogue *(William Washington [6], Thomas Franklin [5], William Thomas [4], William (Col.) [3], John [2], Robert [1])* was born on 18 Oct 1867 in Crittenden County Kentucky, died on 26 Sep 1952 in Caldwell County Kentucky at age 84, and was buried in Frances Presbyterian Church Cemetery Frances Crittenden County Kentucky.

General Notes: M.F. POGUE
Representative Seventh District
MARION FORREST POGUE Representative Seventh District Fredonia Crittenden county District Crittenden and Livingston counties Democrat Farmer merchant Born in Crittenden county October 18 1867 a son of William W and Catherine Pogue Educated in public schools and Marion Academy and Normal School Married Miss Bettie F Matthews in 1887 Taught in the common schools for more than twenty years Member of 1902 House and Assistant Clerk of House 1903 1905 1907 Elected to present house over HE Worton Republican by 375 majority

Marion married **Bettie Florence Matthews,** daughter of **John Matthews** and **Nancy M. Walker,** on 18 Apr 1887 in Crittenden County Kentucky. Bettie was born on 10 Nov 1868 in Crittenden County Kentucky, died on 29 Feb 1952 in Caldwell County Kentucky at age 83, and was buried in Frances Presbyterian Church Cemetery Frances Crittenden County Kentucky.

Children from this marriage were:
+ 57 F i. **Clara Augusta Pogue** was born on 12 May 1888 in Crittenden County Kentucky and died in Aug 1936 in Manila, Mississippi County Arkansas at age 48.

+ 58 M ii. **Forrest Carlisle Pogue Sr** was born on 20 Aug 1889 in Crittenden County Kentucky, died on 29 Oct 1946 in Crittenden County Kentucky at age 57, and was buried in Frances Presbyterian Church Cemetery Frances Crittenden County Kentucky.

Eighth Generation (5th Great-Grandchildren)

57. Clara Augusta Pogue *(Marion Forrest [7], William Washington [6], Thomas Franklin [5], William Thomas [4], William (Col.) [3], John [2], Robert [1])* was born on 12 May 1888 in Crittenden County Kentucky and died in Aug 1936 in Manila, Mississippi County Arkansas at age 48.

Noted events in her life were:
• Cause of Death: colon cancer.

Clara married **Vernon Richard Fox,** son of **Charles Wesley Fox** and **Juliet Hodge,** in 1909 in Crittenden County Kentucky. Vernon was born on 2 May 1884 in Lebanon, Marion County, Kentucky and died in May 1968 in Manila, Mississippi County Arkansas at age 84.

(Duplicate Line. See Person 23 on Page 22)

58. Forrest Carlisle Pogue Sr *(Marion Forrest [7], William Washington [6], Thomas Franklin [5], William Thomas [4], William (Col.) [3], John [2], Robert [1])* was born on 20 Aug 1889 in Crittenden County Kentucky, died on 29 Oct 1946 in Crittenden County Kentucky at age 57, and was buried in Frances Presbyterian Church Cemetery Frances Crittenden County Kentucky.

Descendants of Robert Pogue (Poage)

Forrest married **Fannye C.** Fannye was born in 1891 and died on 19 Dec 1945 in Crittenden County Kentucky at age 54.

The child from this marriage was:

59 M   i.   **Forrest Carlisle Pogue Jr** was born on 17 Sep 1912 in Frances Crittenden County Kentucky, died on 6 Oct 1996 in Frances Crittenden County Kentucky at age 84, and was buried in Frances Presbyterian Church Cemetery Frances Crittenden County Kentucky.

General Notes: Writer. A historian of merit, Forrest C. Pogue, Jr. was born in the rural Crittenden County, Kentucky community of Frances in 1912. A 1931 graduate of Murray State University in Murray, Kentucky, Pogue went on to earn a Ph.D. by the age of 24. He was fluent in French and an expert at the collection of oral history. Historian and author, Stephen E. Ambrose called him "One of the smartest individuals in the US Army." During World War II, he served as an official U.S. Army historian and closely followed combat troops during the D-Day invasion. He was positioned on a hospital ship located at Omaha Beach and interviewed the wounded soldiers who were brought there. His interviews and notes from the war were later published in the work "Pogue's War: Diaries of a World War II Combat Historian." His most significant work was the multi-volume, critically acclaimed authorized biography of famed General George C. Marshall. Pogue spent countless hours personally interviewing General Marshall in preparation for this momentous biographical work. Today, it stands as a landmark in both oral and World War II history. In addition to his writing, Pogue also lectured extensively about his experiences at universities across the nation, among which was West Point Military Academy. The Forrest C. Pogue Public History Institute at Murray State University was named so in his honor.

Forrest married **Christine Brown**. Christine was born on 27 Jun 1914 in Fulton County Kentucky, died on 15 Jun 2010 in Crittenden County Kentucky at age 95, and was buried in Frances Presbyterian Church Cemetery Frances Crittenden County Kentucky.

First Generation

60. Robert Hubbard was born in 1600 in London, Middlesex, , England and died on 9 Feb 1663 in James City, Virginia at age 63.

Robert married **Margaret Kevell** in 1626 in England. Margaret was born in 1606 in East London, England and died in 1644 in England at age 38.

The child from this marriage was:
+ 61 M   i. **Matthew Hubbard** was born in 1627 in Skimino, York, Virginia and died on 24 Apr 1667 in York County, Virginia at age 40.

Second Generation (Children)

61. Matthew Hubbard *(Robert [1])* was born in 1627 in Skimino, York, Virginia and died on 24 Apr 1667 in York County, Virginia at age 40.

Matthew married **Sibella Caynehoe** in 1661 in Williamsburg, James, Virginia. Sibella was born in 1631 in England and died in 1665 in York County, Virginia at age 34.

The child from this marriage was:
+ 62 M   i. **John Hubbard** was born in 1661 in York County Virginia and died in 1726 in New Kent County Virginia at age 65.

Third Generation (Grandchildren)

62. John Hubbard *(Matthew [2], Robert [1])* was born in 1661 in York County Virginia and died in 1726 in New Kent County Virginia at age 65.

John married **Elizabeth** in 1675. Elizabeth was born in 1663 in Virginia and died in 1690 in New Kent County Virginia at age 27.

The child from this marriage was:
+ 63 M   i. **John Hubbard** was born in 1680 in Amelia County, Virginia and died in 1745 in Amelia County, Virginia at age 65.

Fourth Generation (Great-Grandchildren)

63. John Hubbard *(John [3], Matthew [2], Robert [1])* was born in 1680 in Amelia County, Virginia and died in 1745 in Amelia County, Virginia at age 65.

John married **Mary Harrison,** daughter of **John Harrison** and **Mary Ann Willinson,** in 1706 in Caroline County, Virginia. Mary was born in 1680 in Caroline County, Virginia and died in 1780 in Caroline County, Virginia at age 100.

The child from this marriage was:
+ 64 M   i. **George Hubbard** was born in 1723 in Caroline County, Virginia and died in 1820 in Charles City, Viginia at age 97.

Fifth Generation (Great Great-Grandchildren)

64. George Hubbard *(John [4], John [3], Matthew [2], Robert [1])* was born in 1723 in Caroline County, Virginia and died in 1820 in Charles City, Viginia at age 97.

George married **Judith Crew** in 1743-1744 in Caroline County Maryland. Judith was born in 1721 in Charles City, Viginia and died in Charles City, Viginia.

The child from this marriage was:
+ 65 M   i. **John Hubbard** was born on 30 Jul 1752 in Deep River, Guilford, North Carolina and died on 27 Mar 1834 in Deep River, Guilford, North Carolina at age 81.

Sixth Generation (3rd Great-Grandchildren)

65. John Hubbard *(George ^{5}, John ^{4}, John ^{3}, Matthew ^{2}, Robert ^{1})* was born on 30 Jul 1752 in Deep River, Guilford, North Carolina and died on 27 Mar 1834 in Deep River, Guilford, North Carolina at age 81.

John married **Martha Sanders**. Martha was born on 17 Jan 1759 in Deep River, Guilford, North Carolina and died on 23 Mar 1801 in Deep River, Guilford, North Carolina at age 42.

The child from this marriage was:

+ 66 M   i.   **George Hubbard** was born on 14 Apr 1786 in Deep River, Guilford, North Carolina, died on 19 Oct 1865 in Monrovia, Morgan County, Indiana at age 79, and was buried in West Union Cemetery, Monrovia, Morgan County, Indiana.

Seventh Generation (4th Great-Grandchildren)

66. George Hubbard *(John ^{6}, George ^{5}, John ^{4}, John ^{3}, Matthew ^{2}, Robert ^{1})* was born on 14 Apr 1786 in Deep River, Guilford, North Carolina, died on 19 Oct 1865 in Monrovia, Morgan County, Indiana at age 79, and was buried in West Union Cemetery, Monrovia, Morgan County, Indiana.

George married **Nancy A. Huckleberry**. Nancy was born on 28 May 1786 in Rowan County North Carolina and died on 28 Dec 1866 in Monrovia, Morgan County, Indiana at age 80.

The child from this marriage was:

+ 67 M   i.   **John Shields Hubbard** was born on 22 Sep 1811 in Guilford County, North Carolina and died on 31 Dec 1846 in Angel Indian Mounds at age 35.

Eighth Generation (5th Great-Grandchildren)

67. John Shields Hubbard *(George ^{7}, John ^{6}, George ^{5}, John ^{4}, John ^{3}, Matthew ^{2}, Robert ^{1})* was born on 22 Sep 1811 in Guilford County, North Carolina and died on 31 Dec 1846 in Angel Indian Mounds at age 35.

John married **Polly May Hay**, daughter of **Johann Adam Hay** and **Rachel**. Polly was born on 28 Aug 1804 and died on 31 Mar 1847 in Vanderburgh County, IN Reese Williams Cemetery Warrick County IN at age 42.

Children from this marriage were:

+ 68 M   i.   **Jonathan Hubbard** was born about 1830 in Evansville, Vanderburgh County, Indiana and died before 1880 in Evansville, Vanderburgh County, Indiana.

+ 69 M   ii.   **Jesse Golden Hubbard** was born in 1840, died on 23 Dec 1919 in Evansville, Vanderburgh County, Indiana at age 79, and was buried in Oak Hill Cemetery.

Ninth Generation (6th Great-Grandchildren)

68. Jonathan Hubbard *(John Shields ^{8}, George ^{7}, John ^{6}, George ^{5}, John ^{4}, John ^{3}, Matthew ^{2}, Robert ^{1})* was born about 1830 in Evansville, Vanderburgh County, Indiana and died before 1880 in Evansville, Vanderburgh County, Indiana.

Jonathan married **Eliza Louisa Noble**, daughter of **Hager**, on 2 Oct 1868 in Orange County, Indiana. Eliza was born in 1837 in Indiana, died on 7 Sep 1906 in Evansville, Vanderburgh County, Indiana at age 69, and was buried in Oak Hill Cemetery.

Children from this marriage were:

70 M   i.   **Richard P. Hubbard** was born on 5 Feb 1863 in Evansville, Vanderburgh County, Indiana, died on 28 Mar 1930 in Evansville, Vanderburgh County, Indiana at age 67, and was buried in Oak Hill Cemetery.

71 F   ii.   **Cora Hubbard** was born on 13 Nov 1869 in Vanderburgh County, Indiana and died on 22 Jun 1940 in Evansville, Vanderburgh County, Indiana at age 70.

+ 72 M   iii.   **Thomas Hubbard** was born on 4 Dec 1874 in Pigeon, Vanderburgh County, Indiana, died on 30 Jul 1939 in Evansville, Vanderburgh, Indiana at age 64, and was buried in Oak Hill Cemetery.

69. Jesse Golden Hubbard *(John Shields ^{8}, George ^{7}, John ^{6}, George ^{5}, John ^{4}, John ^{3}, Matthew ^{2}, Robert ^{1})* was born in 1840, died on 23 Dec 1919 in Evansville, Vanderburgh County, Indiana at age 79, and was buried in Oak Hill Cemetery.

General Notes: Name: Jessie G. Hubbard
Date: 23 Dec 1919

Descendants of Robert Hubbard

Location:	Knight Township
Age:	83 Yr
Gender:	Male
Race:	White
Source Location:	County Health Office, Evansville
Source notes:	The source of this record is the book H-16 on page 82 within the series produced by the Indiana Works Progress Administration.

Jesse married **Anna Jane Carney**, daughter of **John Carney** and **Melvina Angel**. Anna was born on 16 Nov 1846 in North Carolina, died on 29 May 1929 in Evansville, Vanderburgh County, Indiana at age 82, and was buried in Oak Hill Cemetery.

The child from this marriage was:

   73 M   i.   **William J. Hubbard** was born on 28 Jun 1867 in Evansville, Vanderburgh County, Indiana, died on 1 Jul 1935 in Evansville, Vanderburgh County, Indiana at age 68, and was buried in Oak Hill Cemetery.

      William married **Mabel C. Billingsley**, daughter of **Jacob Billingsley** and **Arvilla Riggs,** on 12 Apr 1893. Mabel was born on 16 Aug 1871 in Cincinatti, Hamilton County Ohio, died on 13 Mar 1949 in Evansville, Vanderburgh County, Indiana at age 77, and was buried in Oak Hill Cemetery.

Tenth Generation (7th Great-Grandchildren)

72. Thomas Hubbard *(Jonathan [9], John Shields [8], George [7], John [6], George [5], John [4], John [3], Matthew [2], Robert [1])* was born on 4 Dec 1874 in Pigeon, Vanderburgh County, Indiana, died on 30 Jul 1939 in Evansville, Vanderburgh, Indiana at age 64, and was buried in Oak Hill Cemetery.

Thomas married **Lena Laubner**, daughter of **John George Laubner** and **Mary Maria Kaiser**. Lena was born on 8 Jul 1876 in Indiana, died on 28 Sep 1938 in Evansville, Vanderburgh County, Indiana at age 62, and was buried in Oak Hill Cemetery.

Children from this marriage were:

 + 74 M   i.   **Marvin Dean Hubbard** was born on 11 Mar 1903 in Evansville, Vanderburgh County, Indiana, died on 16 Dec 1963 in Evansville, Vanderburgh County, Indiana at age 60, and was buried in Oak Hill Cemetery.

   75 M   ii.   **Orville Hubbard** was born about 1905 in Evansville, Vanderburgh County, Indiana.

   76 M iii.   **Ora Dale Hubbard** was born on 15 Feb 1908 in Evansville, Vanderburgh County, Indiana.

   77 F   iv.   **Ruth Marion Hubbard** was born on 10 Jun 1913 in Evansville, Vanderburgh County, Indiana.

   78 M   v.   **Robert Merle Hubbard** was born on 10 Jun 1913 in Evansville, Vanderburgh County, Indiana.

11th Generation (8th Great-Grandchildren)

74. Marvin Dean Hubbard *(Thomas [10], Jonathan [9], John Shields [8], George [7], John [6], George [5], John [4], John [3], Matthew [2], Robert [1])* was born on 11 Mar 1903 in Evansville, Vanderburgh County, Indiana, died on 16 Dec 1963 in Evansville, Vanderburgh County, Indiana at age 60, and was buried in Oak Hill Cemetery.

General Notes: INDIANA WAGONER 114 AM IN 39 DIV

Marvin married **Lydia Wagner**, daughter of **Jacob Wagner** and **Julia M. Pfingston**. Lydia was born in 1900 in Campbell, Warrick County, Indiana, died in 1957 in Manila, Mississippi County, Arkansas at age 57, and was buried in Manila Cemetery.

Descendants of Robert Hubbard

The child from this marriage was:
+ 79   F   i.   **Marion Francis Hubbard** was born on 17 Dec 1923 in Evansville, Vanderburgh County, Indiana, died on 3 Mar 2012 in Lenoir City Loudon County Tennessee at age 88, and was buried in Manila Cemetery.

12th Generation (9th Great-Grandchildren)

79. Marion Francis Hubbard *(Marvin Dean [11], Thomas [10], Jonathan [9], John Shields [8], George [7], John [6], George [5], John [4], John [3], Matthew [2], Robert [1])* was born on 17 Dec 1923 in Evansville, Vanderburgh County, Indiana, died on 3 Mar 2012 in Lenoir City Loudon County Tennessee at age 88, and was buried in Manila Cemetery.

> General Notes: Marion Francis Fox
> Monday, March 26, 2012

Mrs. Marion Francis Fox, 88, of Lenoir City, Tenn., formerly of Manila, passed away Saturday, March 3, 2012, in Lenoir City. Mrs. Fox was born Dec. 17, 1923, in Evansville, Ind., the only child of Marvin and Lydia Wagner Hubbard. She was a 1942 graduate of Cass Technical High School in Detroit, Mich. She married her beloved William G. "Billy" Fox on Feb. 20, 1943, and had been married for 64 years when he passed away. During her years in Manila, Mrs. Fox was Superintendent of Sunday School at First United Methodist Church, a communion steward, usher and Sunday school teacher. She also started the Cub Scouts. In Lenoir City she was a member of the United Methodist Women and the Volunteers Sunday School Class at Central United Methodist Church.

Survivors include two sons, Gary Fox and wife Barbara of Lenoir City and Rick Fox and wife Joy of Anna, Ill.; six grandchildren, Angela Fox and husband Charles Hooker, Kristin-Fox Trautman and husband Lucas, Captain Jonathan Fox and wife Jennifer, Jessica Flinn and husband Michael, Candace Capps and husband Kent, Beth Putman; and 10 great-grandchildren, Myra Trautman, Leia Trautman, Auden Fox, Sophie Putman, Jack Putman, Lydia Capps, Jude Capps, Hudson Capps, Kathleen Fox and William Fox.

Graveside funeral services will be held at 1:30 p.m. Saturday, March 31, at Manila Cemetery under the direction of Howard Funeral Service of Manila.

The family prefers any memorials be made to Central United Methodist Church in Lenoir City or First United Methodist in Manila.

Guest register is www.howardfuneralservice.com.
Obituary courtesy of Northeast Arkansas Town Crier

Marion married **William Garrad Fox,** son of **Vernon Richard Fox** and **Clara Augusta Pogue,** on 20 Feb 1943 in Detroit, Wayne, Michigan. William was born on 21 Aug 1918 in Manila, Mississippi County, Arkansas, died on 14 Nov 2007 in Lenoir City, Loudon County, Tennessee at age 89, and was buried in Manila Cemetery.

(Duplicate Line. See Person 27 on Page 22)

Descendants of Casper Kaiser

First Generation

80. Casper Kaiser was born in 1793 in Germany, died on 6 Oct 1865 in Evansville, Vanderburgh County, Indiana at age 72, and was buried in Saint Joseph Catholic Cemetery.

Casper married **Margaretha**. Margaretha was born in 1791, died on 22 Oct 1858 in Evansville, Vanderburgh County, Indiana at age 67, and was buried in Saint Joseph Catholic Cemetery.

The child from this marriage was:

+ 81 M i. **Francis Kaiser** was born about 1821 in Germany, died on 15 Apr 1874 in Evansville, Vanderburgh County, Indiana about age 53, and was buried in Saint Joseph Catholic Cemetery.

Second Generation (Children)

81. Francis Kaiser *(Casper [1])* was born about 1821 in Germany, died on 15 Apr 1874 in Evansville, Vanderburgh County, Indiana about age 53, and was buried in Saint Joseph Catholic Cemetery.

Francis married **Barbara Brenner**. Barbara was born in 1820 in Germany and died on 16 Apr 1876 in Evansville, Vanderburgh County, Indiana at age 56.

The child from this marriage was:

+ 82 F i. **Mary Maria Kaiser** was born about 1847 in Vanderburgh County, Indiana, died on 6 Jul 1881 in Evansville, Vanderburgh County, Indiana about age 34, and was buried in Saint Joseph Catholic Cemetery.

Third Generation (Grandchildren)

82. Mary Maria Kaiser *(Francis [2], Casper [1])* was born about 1847 in Vanderburgh County, Indiana, died on 6 Jul 1881 in Evansville, Vanderburgh County, Indiana about age 34, and was buried in Saint Joseph Catholic Cemetery.

Mary married **John George Laubner** about 1874 in Evansville, Vanderburgh County, Indiana. John was born about 1842 in Hesse, Germany, died on 5 Nov 1902 in Evansville, Vanderburgh County, Indiana about age 60, and was buried in Oak Hill Cemetery.

Children from this marriage were:

83 M i. **Edward Laubner** was born in Aug 1873 in Indiana.

+ 84 F ii. **Lena Laubner** was born on 8 Jul 1876 in Indiana, died on 28 Sep 1938 in Evansville, Vanderburgh County, Indiana at age 62, and was buried in Oak Hill Cemetery.

85 F iii. **Mary Laubner** was born in 1878, died on 24 Mar 1956 in Vandeburgh County, Indiana at age 78, and was buried in Oak Hill Cemetery.

Mary married **Simpson**.

Mary next married **Harry L. Luton** on 5 Oct 1912 in Vandeburgh County, Indiana.

86 F iv. **Carrie Laubner** was born in Apr 1880 in Indiana.

Fourth Generation (Great-Grandchildren)

84. Lena Laubner *(Mary Maria Kaiser [3], Francis [2], Casper [1])* was born on 8 Jul 1876 in Indiana, died on 28 Sep 1938 in Evansville,

Descendants of Casper Kaiser

Vanderburgh County, Indiana at age 62, and was buried in Oak Hill Cemetery.

Lena married **Thomas Hubbard**, son of **Jonathan Hubbard** and **Eliza Louisa Noble**. Thomas was born on 4 Dec 1874 in Pigeon, Vanderburgh County, Indiana, died on 30 Jul 1939 in Evansville, Vanderburgh, Indiana at age 64, and was buried in Oak Hill Cemetery.

(Duplicate Line. See Person 72 on Page 33)

Descendants of Joseph Wagner

First Generation

87. Joseph Wagner was born on 6 Nov 1812 in Alsace-Lorraine, died on 22 Nov 1893 in Elberfeld, Warrick County, Indiana at age 81, and was buried in Saint John Catholic Cemetery.

Joseph married **Catharine Elmerich**. Catharine was born on 25 Nov 1817 in Alsace-Lorraine, died on 7 Dec 1893 in Elberfeld, Warrick County, Indiana at age 76, and was buried in Saint John Catholic Cemetery.

Children from this marriage were:

88 M   i.   **Charles Wagner** was born on 17 Jun 1841 in Ohio, died on 26 Oct 1912 in Warrick County, Indiana at age 71, and was buried in Saint John Catholic Cemetery.

89 F   ii.   **Julia Wagner** was born about 1844 in Ohio.

90 M   iii. **Joseph Wagner** was born about 1846 in Ohio.

91 M   iv.   **Anthony Wagner** was born on 4 Jul 1847 in Ohio, died on 6 Jul 1900 in Elberfeld, Warrick County, Indiana at age 53, and was buried in Saint John Catholic Cemetery.

92 M   v.   **John Wagner** was born about 1849 in Ohio.

93 M   vi.   **Leo Wagner** was born about 1852 in Campbell, Warrick County, Indiana.

94 M   vii. **Lafayette Wagner** was born about 1854 in Campbell, Warrick County, Indiana.

95 M   viii. **George C. Wagner** was born on 4 Jan 1861 in Warrick County, Indiana, died on 16 May 1948 in Vanderburgh County, Indiana at age 87, and was buried in Saint John Catholic Cemetery.

+ 96 M ix.   **Jacob Wagner** was born in Mar 1863 in Elberfeld, Warrick County, Indiana, died on 11 Mar 1931 in Elberfeld, Warrick County, Indiana at age 68, and was buried in Saint John Catholic Cemetery.

97 M   x.   **Adam Frank Wagner** was born on 29 Sep 1868 in Campbell, Warrick County, Indiana, died on 11 Mar 1951 in Evansville, Vanderburgh County, Indiana at age 82, and was buried in Saint Joseph Catholic Cemetery.

Second Generation (Children)

96. Jacob Wagner *(Joseph [1])* was born in Mar 1863 in Elberfeld, Warrick County, Indiana, died on 11 Mar 1931 in Elberfeld, Warrick County, Indiana at age 68, and was buried in Saint John Catholic Cemetery.

Jacob married **Julia M. Pfingston**, daughter of **Henry Pfingston** and **Elizabeth Christian**. Julia was born on 5 Feb 1870 in Germany, died on 18 Mar 1958 in Evansville, Vanderburgh County, Indiana at age 88, and was buried in Saint Joseph Catholic Cemetery.

Children from this marriage were:

    98 M   i.   **Otto C. Wagner** was born on 12 Nov 1889 in Indiana and died in Jun 1984 in Evansville, Vanderburgh County, Indiana at age 94.

    99 M   ii. **Albert Wagner** was born on 12 Aug 1891 in Campbell, Warrick, Indiana and died in Dec 1975 in Evansville, Vanderburgh County, Indiana at age 84.

  100 M   iii. **Ralph Wagner** was born on 18 Jun 1893 and died in Oct 1973 in San Rafael, Marin, California at age 80.

  101 F   iv. **Marie E. Wagner** was born on 29 May 1897 in Elberfeld, Warrick County, Indiana and died on 5 Dec 1969 in Evansville, Vanderburgh County, Indiana at age 72.

+ 102 F   v.   **Lydia Wagner** was born in 1900 in Campbell, Warrick County, Indiana, died in 1957 in Manila, Mississippi County, Arkansas at age 57, and was buried in Manila Cemetery.

Third Generation (Grandchildren)

102. Lydia Wagner *(Jacob [2], Joseph [1])* was born in 1900 in Campbell, Warrick County, Indiana, died in 1957 in Manila, Mississippi County, Arkansas at age 57, and was buried in Manila Cemetery.

Lydia married **Marvin Dean Hubbard**, son of **Thomas Hubbard** and **Lena Laubner**. Marvin was born on 11 Mar 1903 in Evansville, Vanderburgh County, Indiana, died on 16 Dec 1963 in Evansville, Vanderburgh County, Indiana at age 60, and was buried in Oak Hill Cemetery.

(Duplicate Line. See Person 74 on Page 33)

Lydia next married **Milam**.

Name Index

Name Index

Willinson

Mary Ann, 18, 31

Winn

Mary Cox, 4

Woodson

Christian, 12, 25